Saving Our Pennys

Roy Dimond

&

Jeff Leitch

Concord, New Hampshire

Saving Our Pennys
by
Roy Dimond and Jeff Leitch

Paperback ISBN 13: 978-1-61807-112-5
Mobi (Kindle) ISBN 13: 978-1-61807-113-2
ePub (Sony, Nook, iPad) ISBN 13: 978-1-61807-114-9
Library of Congress Control Number (LOC): 2013955067

Cover & Interior Design:
Pamela Marin-Kingsley, Grey Gate Media, LLC

TaoFish Books
an imprint of Grey Gate Media LLC
Concord, New Hampshire
Email: info@greygatemedia.com
Website: www.greygatemedia.com

To our families, whom we cherish,
To our wives, who are our best friends,
To our mothers, who both passed before their time,
To our fathers, who are the greatest role models sons could have.

For Ian,
One of the "Lads"
Who makes all
Teaching Days Better.
I'm lucky to know you.

Lads together

Jeff Geitel

Introduction

It is an honor to work with you.
~The Apprentice

I first met Roy at university during my Professional Development Program for Education. In a world versed in theory, Roy came in and breathed the life of practice into us. Even today, people believe his talk was the most defining moment of their practicum. He only spoke to us for an hour! I realized that this man was bringing more to the educational forum than just a glimpse of concern about kids. He talked of passion, of questioning why we were working with students, what gave us the right to teach and what will we offer them. He asked us if we believed in hope.

With great fortune in my own life, I would have the opportunity in my first year of teaching to work at the same school as Roy. In my fifth and sixth years of teaching, we worked together in the same department alongside "at-risk" youth. I was amazed as I watched him walk with students on their life's journey, never walking ahead or behind them, but only beside. If these students fell, Roy patiently waited for them to rise, and if they said, "I can't." Roy said, "Yes you can, I believe in you." The message is poignantly clear, but you will have to walk with us inside these pages to *see for yourself.*

How do you define a mentor? Someone who is an

experienced and trusted friend? An adviser? I would like to think it is someone who leads through the committed practice of compassion with the intention of understanding identity, all the while cloaking it with hope. If you look under that cloak, you will see the face of Roy Dimond.

Thank you Roy, it has been an honor.

Jeff

You are my friend, you can do no wrong.
~The Mentor

I was privileged to meet Jeff while speaking at the university he attended. After I finished my presentation, he approached with a crowd of people. He had a thousand questions but asked only one, then stood aside so others could speak. That was my first impression of Jeff, small ego, humble.

Coincidentally, in his first year of teaching, he was assigned to my school. Over time, Jeff asked his thousand questions and I answered them to the best of my ability. Often these questions challenged me to reflect upon my mentor's teachings and for that, I am grateful. Our relationship deepened and soon the word friend became part of our vocabulary. One true loss in my life is that I never introduced Jeff to my guide, my ferryman, the man who mentored me. He died just after Jeff and I met, but his words are carried in my heart—everyday. There is a line of consciousness from my mentor through me, to Jeff, and in time, to whomever he is asked to guide. That student may appear as his own child, a colleague seeking mastery or a stranger on a quest. Their search for him has already begun.

I believe we were destined to write this book. As you walk through these pages with us, remember these words from The Gatekeeper. *"You have eyes... use them."*

Oh, and one other thing. Lab really did live!

Namaste!

Roy

Prologue

Before enlightenment
chopping wood
carrying water.

After enlightenment
chopping wood
carrying water.

~Zen Proverb

As an apprentice, the accurate description of me is that I am a "Shadow." I am neither proud nor ashamed of this. I am a teacher, but what I offer could easily be experienced by anyone, no matter his or her calling.

My life is one of quality. I have a good marriage, a fulfilling job, and so therefore no intention to change. Despite this, or possibly because of it, another entity deep within me struggles to exist.

First however, before that entity can manifest, I must experience the in-between, that moment between unconsciousness and consciousness. In this time called choice, one moves from "Shadow" to "Substance."

Then, if earned, an epiphany will move one from "Substance" to "Spirit." You will know when this happens by the things that become important to you. However, before all this, comes the great harbinger of change... dread!

Shadow: A mere semblance [a shadow of his former self] something insubstantial, [worn to a shadow], an inseparable companion...

Each season has its ending and beginning; each age has its changes and transformations; misery and happiness regularly alternate. Here our views are thwarted, and yet the result may afterwards have our approval; there we insist on our own views, and looking at things differently from others, try to correct them, while we are in error ourselves.
~Chuang Tzu

Chapter 1

There are no special doors for calamity and happiness; they come as men themselves call them. Their recompenses follow good and evil as the shadow follows the substance.
~The Thai-Shang

In classrooms everywhere there is a sacred moment that society does not know. Students and parents are also unaware. Only teachers understand. It does not matter if you have taught for twenty years, or it is your very first day on the job. It does not matter if you teach in an American inner city or a grass hut in Africa. All teachers experience it.

Upon walking into class at the beginning of each year, before anyone else arrives, you are intensely aware of it. Sitting in each desk, thunderous in the quiet, pulsating with excitement, waiting for its child, is a power called potential!

I relish the pure simplicity of that moment. With desks in straight rows, books all in their place, my teacher's desk uncluttered, there is hope.

So here I sit, looking out over the rows of apparently empty desks expecting another year like any other.

I became a teacher to help others fulfill their potential

– but, ironically, I never visualize my own. My life has become all about what others might accomplish. This time, however, something is struggling within and in the silence it whispers: "Not this year."

Still, the reaffirming smiles from administrators and colleagues feel good. While walking through empty halls, the walls shudder with the forgotten energy of ghost children. I am blissfully unaware that calamity and happiness bring forth change. Little do I know that this is the year I will discover in me that which is most human.

Relaxing, I feel a sense of control knowing that I am prepared for the upcoming year. Unacknowledged, however, is that each year my energy level for the job seems subtly less. How am I to last in a profession for thirty years, when it already feels like I have worked that long? It's only my third year!

While organizing and preparing my classroom, I contemplate how every objective criterion reinforces that I am a good teacher. Administrators have requested me for their schools, colleagues occasionally search out advice, and parents regularly praise me. Even some of the children like me.

While I walk to the bookroom, ghost children continue their conversations. I can almost hear their bellowing. Every greeting mixes with nervous laughter and false bravado. These halls have vibrated with such sounds for generations. Tomorrow, real students will replace these memories.

By the end of the day I am prepared, and look forward to the coming year. Still, there is something niggling at me.

After carrying boxes out to my jeep, I slide in behind the steering wheel and look forward to the drive home. I follow the same route as I have for three years—when suddenly irritation crushes down upon me. Anxiety grips the steering wheel, and I watch my knuckles turn white. I had left work prepared and relaxed, and yet—as so often before – I'm returning home frustrated and tense. I blame the other drivers, but do I actually grant strangers ownership of my emotions? Since I have so much going for me, I have to stop allowing others' unconsciousness to upset me. If I'm having such a great life, then I must not allow someone who isn't to affect me. When a driver cuts me off and gives me the obligatory finger, it's embarrassing how quickly I go to their level. I should be above this, but I cannot seem to rise from the muck. Why do I live a life of reaction? Adding to my anxiety is the knowledge that a day beginning so full of promise should end that way.

Even during summer vacation these unidentified feelings filter through. I've always used summer for quality family time, and to recharge. At the beginning of holidays, not having my life ruled by schedules, bells and meetings is almost unfathomable. While enjoying this golden time, I often think about my accomplishments. As Socrates once said, "An unexamined life is a wasted life." None of this, however, helps me comprehend what these feelings are, or from where they come.

Chapter 2

Home is not where you live
But where they understand you.
~Christian Morgenstern

I worry that my wife detects an aura of anxiety about me, but she writes it off to my understandable need to hang on to the last days of summer. Sadly, I know it is something much deeper. I am always fighting off a sense of fatigue, and often wonder if this is what leads to my reacting all the time. A famous football coach once said, "Fatigue makes cowards of us all." Was I a coward? Time will tell.

I live just outside the city that I teach in, with my three children, wife and dog, in a small log home. We prefer the intimacy of a modest house, as it forces interactions. Our dog has an unusual amount of dog DNA, meaning that he acts more dog-like than any canine I have ever known. It's impossible to know what he is thinking unless food, belly scratches, or walks are involved. Then his tail speaks volumes. He's a Labrador, and his name is Lab. He doesn't like swimming or, for that matter even walking in the rain. I know this because anytime a raindrop has the audacity to touch him... he winces. He makes up for this, "unlab" behavior by sprawling in front of the fire whenever possible. He also has a Labrador smile that can be most unnerving, especially when I share my intimate concerns.

My three children are at an age of wonderment. Santa remains real, the Tooth Fairy is watched for and they still see me as Superman. This, I am sure, will never change.

My wife is my soul mate. She understands me and yet still loves me. She's an evolved woman—some would say a saint.

Whenever I share any of this with Lab, he grins sardonically.

Our community is more forest than pavement. We have a few acres where the neighbors are near, and yet we have privacy. Deer sleep next to our house and wolves howl from the distant mountains. Life is tranquil.

Traditionally, on the last day before the start of school, we all drag the canoe to the lake for one last paddle. We do this at dusk, just as the light changes. We paddle to the middle of the lake and then sit, bobbing along. The dimming dusk turns to vibrant sunset, then a loon circles the lake calling his family home, and finally darkness descends. We watch for stars and simply experience the moment. Every year, I wish we could freeze our moment forever. I understand my family and they understand me.

Chapter 3

**The mind is not a vessel to be filled,
but a fire to be ignited.
~Plutarch**

Finally, it has arrived. The first day of school, and I am both excited and exhausted. I didn't sleep well last night, not because of anticipation but because of the daunting energy that will soon focus upon me. The paper work and administrivia is overwhelming. Added to this is the industry's focus to get the paperwork done as quickly as possible. This always leaves an uncomfortable tone of nagging in the school.

I used to learn the names of my students quickly, but no longer. There are too many.

A bell shrieks and feet stomp. The horde moves. They pile into class, understandably more interested in one another than me. I have no time to greet them, or properly introduce myself because the paperwork demands attention.

I could rationalize the sore throat that I will have by the end of the first week, but why am I already frustrated? I love being a teacher, but do not love the feelings that teaching gives me.

The staff room is a reaffirming place. My feelings are

reflected in the faces of my peers. Wide eyes greet wide eyes—
one from shock, others just overwhelmed. Some speak in voices
a little too loud, while others grab coffee and search out a quiet
corner. Others are like the children, full of false bravado.

Despite my best efforts to make my classroom welcoming, no one has even noticed. Class after class is the same.
Paperwork, paperwork, and then more paperwork to police
the paperwork that is to be completed. How did computers
increase the use of paper? After the last of my students file out,
I acknowledge that I have completed the tasks... endured... survived. Fulfilling, it is not.

At the end of the day there's a staff meeting. Just like
every other year at this time, we listen to opening remarks
from the principal. Introductions of new staff and updates on
activities over the summer are first on the agenda. It is always
interesting to watch the different shell-shocked cliques. Some
teachers listen attentively. New teachers take notes, some whisper to friends, while most try to complete the day's paperwork.
Staff meetings look like the regular classroom. Pranksters, the
apathetic, jocks, academics and appeasers cluster together for
support.

Individuals stand and make their individual points
regarding their individual agendas, all under the banner: "We
are a team." As one teacher pontificates, more to hear his own
voice than to actually say something of substance, I notice a
teacher has returned to our ranks. She left last year because of
health issues. There are all these life issues with our, "teammates," yet more time is actually given to the fact that the
school is short on soccer coaches. No one acknowledges her
return, and I feel sheepish that I didn't stand and welcome her
back. Something deep within finds this obscene. It feels wrong.

I return home, not exhilarated, but questioning why I
hadn't said, "Glad you're back."

Chapter 4

Alas! The fearful Unbelief is unbelief
in yourself.
~Thomas Carlyle

The next morning, I have the very same thought; why did I not welcome that teacher back? She survives a life-threatening illness, and I do not have it in me to greet her. While I'm driving to work contemplating this, the driver ahead suddenly cuts me off. I slam my brakes, narrowly missing him. He, of course, proceeds to speed through a red light. The driver behind me hits his horn and I explode. Here I am, still shaking from a near accident, and some idiot honks.

Soothing my rage, I give him the traditional finger. I feel better. Then in my rear-view mirror I see his car door open. Anger allows me to take the confrontation to the next level. My hand grips the door handle. Fingers tighten, ready to fling it open. Unexpectedly, a gentle tapping on my window distracts me. Standing beside my car, his posture straight as a sentinel, is...a priest. I let go of the door handle like sliding a gun back into its holster. I roll down my window, and he benignly smiles and apologizes for mistakenly hitting his car horn. I stammer an awkward but very sincere apology.

I began this day the same way that I ended the previous one: sheepish. The rest of my drive to work is spent wondering what kind of punishment there is for giving a priest the finger.

Once I'm at school, the bureaucracy of the beginning school year continues to demand attention. Files, lockers, textbooks, homeroom, statistical information, class schedules, two hundred new students, two hundred new names, family information, doctor's phone numbers, emergency phone numbers, foster parent phone numbers, blended family names and numbers, siblings names, allergies, medical information—all necessary, but also time-consuming and frustrating.

During all this noise, a former student drops in to say, "Hi." She doesn't yet know what she will do now, maybe a job, maybe travel. In between my yelling out locker numbers, she tells me she is still using drugs. She looks okay, but I am sad for her. We have a forced good-bye because I am off to the office to hand in a class list. As I traverse the express route some call a hallway, I feel bad that we didn't have time to talk. Besides, I'll see her again.

I didn't know it at the time, but I never do.

Hopefully, using the office as an off-ramp will be quieter than the freeway I am on. The speed limit drops as I use this tributary to try to conserve my limited energy. This also provides an opportunity to pick up my revised class lists, while dropping off my already outdated class lists, which had been revised only an hour earlier. Apparently this detour is a bad decision, as the vice-principal yells to the crowd milling about the seven secretaries, "Get out of the office unless you have business!" I want to explain that I am just picking up my revised list as requested, but keep my mouth shut and move on. Returning to the overrun, speeding freeway, I realize that less than twenty-four hours ago, administration had asked us to "Drop in and say 'Hi'."

I merge back onto the twelve-lane thoroughfare, and push my way through the crowd. I use the time-tested method of keeping my head down and scowling, and no one exchanges greetings. I turn into an even larger hall, and the speed limit increases. The school is moving at a dizzying rate. I merge lanes trying to get near the wall, and finally make it to the inside lane. Grabbing a handle, I frantically fling open the door and stumble into my classroom.

I immediately apologize to the young boy I nearly knock over, then mutter an insincere acknowledgement to the students who have been waiting. My computer pings an incoming message, so I ignore the rest of the students as they spill into class. As my computer hums, I'm so busy being prepared that I hardly notice them. Class lists need verification and e-mails demand a reaction. This will help the office staff do their chores expediently.

Another frantic teacher comes in and adds to the chaos by grabbing books from over my head. I plant my face in the keyboard to avoid decapitation by a cupboard door. She flutters on about some P. A. announcement and then rushes out. I try to be patient... but no "Excuse me" or acknowledgment, nothing, just a door slamming behind her. I turn to address my class and notice an edge to my voice.

I make the mistake with some students of expecting them to arrive with appropriate materials. Those without pens and paper are instructed to go get them. My expectations may be too high, as two students leave class and never return. Another goes to the library and looks up information on colleges—or, more accurately, Playmates of the North West Conference. Two more find an administrator and complain that their families are on welfare and cannot afford pens and paper.

Just then, the librarian comes bursting into my class

yelling frantically, "Your students are using computers inappropriately!"

At the same time, I get a call from the vice-principal who contemptuously lectures, "How are students to pay for materials if they don't have the money?" I am tempted to hand the telephone to the librarian and see what kind of conversation would ensue.

Instead, I tell the librarian to inform the students how their use of library equipment is improper and I will do the same. I tell the vice-principal that I wish someone had alerted me that the two families are on welfare, and avoid suggesting he ask how they can afford the cigarettes dangling from their pockets. If I ever find the time, I will try to track down the students who went home. I never do.

The bell dismisses class, and like Pavlov's puppies we react. Due to all the interruptions, I do not take attendance. Who exactly was there would be a guess. The remainder of the day is about the same.

Despite this, it has been a good day. Paperwork is complete and assignments are handed out, and I even have a moment to interact with my peers. Besides, the administrators declare the school "Off to a great start."

That night, late in the evening with a glass of port in my hand, I reflect on the start of the year. I have a sense of pride in completing my difficult professional responsibilities, and yet feel empty. How many students had I walked past today? It must have been one or two thousand. I wonder if the student who briefly attended my class last year was still on my list. I think her name was Penny. For the rest of the evening, restless thoughts prevent my relaxation.

The next day speeds past, similar to the previous one. As the first week ends, I have my bureaucratic paperwork complete.

This actually gives me a sense of fulfillment, despite the fact that I still don't know my students' names.

I notice that Penny is on my class list, although I haven't yet actually seen her. This means that she must have completed last year. I do not know her well, but her passing does surprise me. She should be in my last period class today, so I make a mental note to see if she attends.

During lunch, I gobble a sandwich before a knock on the staff room door interrupts. A need calls, and so I respond. Experienced teachers always sit farthest from the staff door. They have learned that whoever sits closest never finishes their lunch due to the non-stop knocking.

When I finally return, I sit... just in time for the bell to clang, "MOVE!" In my head I pretend it is a gentle gong whispering, "When you get a moment... MOVE!" I toss away my unfinished lunch and stand, glancing out the window, where miles away a mountain range cuts jagged across an azure sky. People rush past, and the room shimmers. I sit, or more accurately, find myself sitting... in a cold sweat. I am removed, not part of the parade rushing towards the door. I try to stand, but instead my head turns and through the maze of moving bodies I see one teacher. He is calmly munching a sandwich. He inhales deeply and contently exhales. Somehow, he knows that I am watching him, and through the stampeding arms and legs, our eyes meet. He smiles warmly. My hand presses against my chest and a gas bubble moves. Heartburn, not a heart attack, I muse. I return the smile and stifle a belch. He is so calm.

My colleague rises, saunters against the flow of humanity towards me, and looks down. I am deeply uncomfortable. As the last of the traffic merges onto the freeway, quiet descends. Then my colleague says the oddest thing. "Sometimes I wonder where my shadow is. But then I wait, and it usually catches up.

Breathe deep, my friend, or someday that gas bubble will be the real deal." He then rather casually leaves.

I arrive late for class, and notice for the first time that this same teacher is across the hall. Somehow, he is well into his lesson while I am still getting everyone to settle. While teaching, I notice that Penny is there, but clearly lost with the assignment. With her sporadic attendance, what can she expect?

During class I have confrontations with students, but they happen because I care. I can ignore these incidents, but to have control I must exercise power. I must be seen as a figure of authority. Power means control, and control means that I can teach the curriculum. It takes huge amounts of energy for me to be organized enough so that a proper learning environment is instilled into the fabric of my class.

Just then, I look out my door and see that teacher. He's smiling. It will be months before I have my class under enough control so that I can finally ease up and smile. Just then, a raucous laughter bursts from his class and I notice him doubled over, laughing so hard. I feel dread wash over me, and would have felt better if it had been envy.

At the end of the day, I slump exhausted behind my desk. How many months are we into the school year? Just a week? Impossible! How did that teacher do it? He looks as if he enjoys his job. I never smile until second term. These insecurities are not like me. Just the other day, an administrator called me into the office to "Pat me on the back." He noticed and appreciated that my paperwork was complete. In an odd way it added to my frustration.

Just then the teacher from across the hall meanders over, hands in his pockets as if he didn't have a care in the world. Without asking, he pulls a stool up beside my desk. Again I feel uncomfortable.

"How is the school year starting for you?"

"Great," I answer.

"Good, good." He seems to have the same smile as my Lab. "Well, if you ever need any help, just ask." He quickly pulls the stool out from under himself and saunters towards the door. He is whistling, and for some reason it fills me with a sense of urgency, as if an opportunity has just been offered and I am a coward.

I hear myself ask, "How do you do it?"

Without turning, he responds. "Do what?"

I'm not really sure what I am asking, and an uncomfortable minute passes. At least, uncomfortable for me; he seems fine. Finally, I find my words. "How do you look so relaxed?"

He turns. For the first time I realize he has an extraordinary face. He is in his late fifties, but carries not an ounce of fat. He looks fit, like a boxer. What is extraordinary however, is his nose. The many strange angles reveal that it has been broken several times. He has graying, wavy hair and eyes... yes, it is his eyes... his smile always reaches his eyes, making them look like they're constantly dancing with joy. I have often heard him quoting Chaucer and dozens of other writers from memory while teaching English, yet something tells me that he comes from the mean streets. His Scottish accent gives him a toughness that I would not want to cross, but I know the control he has in his class does not come from a place of intimidation. Yet I cannot discern from where it comes.

He chuckles. "I look so relaxed because I am relaxed."

I stammer. "Oh."

He walks over to the window and gazes out at the mountains, then asks the oddest thing. "Why are you a teacher?"

"I'm sorry?"

"Why do you teach?" He looks at me for a long time, as if he is deciding something enormous. I am decidedly lost and my brain stutters. Too many answers and no answers come to mind.

He asks, "What gives you the right to teach?" His tone does not allow offence, as somehow I know that he is asking from a place of kindness. But still, no definitive answers come. He graciously accepts my silence and pulls the stool back to the side of my desk. "This place," his hand sweeps the room and his eyes glance into the hall, "is a giant train."

I nod, yet do not understand.

"Every September there's a lot of noise. Smoke belches, wheels spin as they grab for momentum. Its very being, its existence, is to move forward. But in the beginning, it doesn't actually go anywhere. It doesn't actually do anything. It just spins its wheels. But in time, suddenly, violently, the wheels catch. A great shudder runs from one end of the train to the other. People jolt with kinetic energy. You with me?"

I nod, but not really.

"Once those wheels start turning, the train begins to move. Very quickly this momentum gathers an energy all its own. Once this happens, a direction is set. Not by the people running the train, nor by the people using the train, but by the need of the energy created by the train." Again he catches me completely by surprise. "Ever wonder why a school has so many secretaries and so few counselors?"

I nod, realizing I have never noticed. Despite asking the question, he does not provide an answer. Apparently he is going to make me think.

"Now, changing direction is no longer an option. The destination of the train and its passengers is now one and the same. We all survive until the end of the school year. Some of the passengers will, however, step off and no one will even notice."

I think of Penny.

Chapter 5

The Tao is near and people seek it far away.
~Mencius

Three weeks into the school year we have a Professional Development Day. Finally, an opportunity to breathe. People mingle in small groups, and I sense their awkwardness. I cannot tell if they are simply hesitant for another nebulous professional day or if it is something else.

Moving through the different clusters, I catch snippets of conversations. Someone asks me, "How is your year going?"

"Great," I answer, but immediately realize that I don't mean it.

Another teacher asks, "I saw Penny in your class yesterday. How is she doing?"

Embarrassed, I respond, "Don't really know. Haven't had time to check on her."

Standing unseen behind me is the teacher with the thick Scottish accent. He startles me by adding, "Too bad. She's an excellent kid."

I am about to say, "I didn't know that," but instead swallow my words.

Another colleague joins us, and she also asks, "How is your year going?"

"Fine," I mutter. Uncomfortable, I excuse myself and pretend to look over the stale pastries that are offered as a breakfast. A teacher has just asked about my year and I answer, "Great," not meaning it. Moments later, the same question—but my answer changes to a lame, "Fine." Which is it?

When asked about Penny, why did I swallow my words? Did pride prevent me from acknowledging that I do not know one of my own students?

Lost in thought, I see the day evaporate before my eyes. I drive home struggling to understand my feelings. The reason that I do not know that Penny is a good kid is because we never talk. I never have the time.

My ego immediately begins rationalizing, trying to dampen these thoughts as quickly as possible. It is not my fault. With all the demands, I cannot keep track of all the quiet, sad, faces that come and go. Am I immune? Desensitized? Unconscious? Why did that Scottish teacher ask why am I a teacher? What gives me the right?

Pulling into the garage, I am again perplexed that a day that has the potential to be so invigorating, or at the very least relaxing, is so draining. Is unconsciousness exhausting me? I try to leave these thoughts in the garage. I drag myself up the stairs and into the kitchen, and notice the calendar. Tomorrow is the first day of autumn. I am also aware of a weight on my shoulders like none experienced before. Unknowingly, I carry dread into my home.

Choice: The power or opportunity to choose, an alternative, a quantity and variety to choose from, the best, of fine quality; excellent; superior.

In our sleep,
Pain which cannot forget
Falls drop by drop
Upon the heart until,
In our own despair
Against our will,
Comes wisdom through the awful
Grace of God.
~Aeschylus

Chapter 6

Look children hailstones!
Let's rush out!
~Basho

There is nothing quite like being in a log home during a storm. The more it rains and the harder it blows, the better the experience. The howling wind brings sounds from far away. With these sounds come thoughts, thoughts whose origins are not so far away. Wind-song first builds in distant treetops, then rolls toward the house. It pushes and shoves its way over, around and through the forest. It gets louder. Then you feel it pound the side of the house, logs flex and the roof ripples. Finally it rolls like a wave over the house and crashes off into the dense forest. A powerful storm rattles your home and shakes your soul. If you should lose electrical power, all the better. Experiencing an autumn storm on a seacoast helps form a consciousness of contemplation.

This weekend, I decide to take it easy and regroup. The only thing to do is attend to pre-storm tasks, get all the chairs off the deck and chop some dry wood. The echo of neighbors stockpiling firewood is oddly reassuring. The last mandatory tasks are to boil water for tea, find the storm candles and grab a good book before the predictable loss of power.

Once the storm hits, it hits hard. Lab lies in his safe spot near the fireplace. When the power flicks off he looks up with his "Lab smile" and releases a contented sigh, then drops his head back on his blanket. Occasionally, when a particularly powerful gust hits, I acknowledge his concern and tell him everything is okay. That is all he needs to hear. My concern however, is not so easily salved. The ferocity of the storm outside may actually match my internal struggle.

With this magnificent storm comes the gift of time, as I am now its prisoner. I use it to contemplate what bothers me. I try to be as objective as possible. Again this year, all the leaders of the school declare it, "A great start." Personally, it is something less than great. It is not just my own issues guiding to this conclusion. The school is more frantic, and getting more so every year. Success is shouted louder, and earlier, and more often, but that does not make it so.

My psyche soothes that it is just taking the educational wheels a little longer to roll. Deep down, however, my intense feeling of dread reveals that I fear something. This partially explains why I am comfortable walking past all the students without even so much as eye contact. At a workshop, I learned how fear-based systems perpetuate. People waste so much time defending a decision based on fear, all the while unconsciously reinforcing that same fear. A Samurai once wrote, "If you have no ego, you have no fear." My mind plays with the words ego and fear, fear and ego. Could they be one and the same?

From this internal dialogue, it comes to me that I need to be more observant of both my colleagues and myself. I am curious if they are functioning from the same place. After years of cutbacks and the vulnerable role teachers have in society, it would be psychologically easy for the entire system to subtly slip to a place of fear. Administrators can call it process and governments may call it accountability, but it is really just fear.

I hope that my ego is not hiding the truth. But to prevent this, I will have to improve my listening skills. It seems that as the noise and chaos in schools increases, people's ability to hear each other decreases. The same can be said for society in general. There are so many new ways for people to communicate, but if there is no one on the other end listening... I have spent a lot of time and energy trying to be heard. Listening might be less energy-draining. Ever so slightly, my sense of dread lifts.

In time the storm passes and, as after most blows, things are well tossed about. While driving away from the house, I glance back to see how it managed. A woodpile is blown over, a few snapped branches, but my home is untouched. The day feels great for the first time in...well, a long time. Yes, the sense of dread is definitely lighter. It's as if the thought of listening has acted like the wind itself, blowing the storm out to sea.

As the last of the purple rain-clouds disappear beyond the horizon, the aroma left behind has a scent of fall. Like the air itself, today is fresh, vibrant. My four-wheel drive grinds over debris left from the storm.

Turning the corner down a country road, I suddenly have to jam on the brakes, skidding to a halt. Wandering across the road in front of me is a family of elk. Mother waits patiently for the little one to wobble across. All legs and snout not yet grown into its body, it gambols across the pavement. Eventually, they pass without incident. Next out of the woods however, crashes the father—all eighteen hundred pounds of him, not counting the antlers that are wider than my jeep. He stops in the middle of the road, twenty meters in front of me and turns his magnificent head. His ears twitch and his hoof paws the road as if to say, "You want a piece of me?" We stare at each other and he gives me a disdainful snort. I lamely hit my horn trying to get him to concede the right of way. Thankfully, he sees me as an unworthy adversary and thunders into the forest after his family.

I step on the gas to continue my journey and almost hit a car that has stopped behind me. Unconsciously, I have slipped my automatic transmission into reverse in case the elk charges. Here the goal of the week is to be more observant, yet not two hundred yards from my house an unconscious act occurs. Interesting.

Chapter 7

We look backward too much and we look
forward too much; thus we miss the only eter-
nity of which we can be absolutely sure—the
eternal present, for it is always now.
~William Phelps

The bell for first period clamors for everyone to, "MOVE!" My
colleagues' eyes cloud over as a veil of survival descends.
Choosing to be more observant might prove to be more difficult
than anticipated. I assumed that it would give me insight, and
have not considered that it might bring pain. The staff room
door opens, and we exit into the chaos of the halls. Noise and
energy envelope all in their path.

Starting first period I feel out of place. I cannot stop
thinking about the sound from last night's storm. The fierce
wind sounded just like an engine, and my Scottish colleague
and his train analogy comes to mind.

Teachers stand by their classes, herding students, and I
can almost hear everyone yelling, "All aboard, last call, everybody all aboard!" But what if you miss the "education train?"
There may or may not be other ones. A different "train" might
lead to an entirely different place, possibly a destination no
passenger deserves. Then suddenly the train pulls out with

whoever has the skills or support to hang on.

Passengers rush to their assigned seats. I hear the all too familiar noise and crush of humanity in the aisle. Even as smoke and noise engulfs the engineers of the education train, they command the wheels to go, and go they do. Again they spin, creating even more noise and smoke. Soon, the predictable forward momentum jerks through the train, forcing everybody to grab onto whatever they can so they don't fail. Engineers declare the start "great," mainly because the train leaves on time.

I look across the hall and my Scottish colleague speaks quietly with his class. They seem to be traveling at a different speed. He is one with his shadow, while my shadow frantically bounces off the walls, and the ceiling, and screams madly down the hall. As I speak, I hear my own voice. It's shrill.

I wonder about the perspective of the passengers left standing on the train's platform. They step off the train for just a moment, to smell a rose or experience a crisis. Does it all appear "great" to them? At the end of the hall I see a student. Doors close as classes begin. She is late. We stare at each other. Left on the platform, she has her head down. She glances up. Her hair hides her face, but it does not hide her tears as they drop to the ground and appear to form a rock wall encircling her. Is this what survival looks like... a hardening heart?

I consider walking to the end of the deserted hall and ask if she needs help but four students are simultaneously asking me questions. My computer pings, the office needs my attendance, the PA squawks announcements that the students should be listening to. I try to slow the train by listening, but all I hear is noise. When I look back, the vision at the end of the hall is gone.

As class ends, I feel oddly disturbed. Usually I focus in class. This daydreaming is unlike me. Sometimes, teaching is like holding a handful of sand. Teachable moments appear, but unless I focus, they just slip through my fingers. Whatever happened to the ex-student, who dropped by the first day of school and mentioned she was doing drugs? What train did she catch after leaving my class? The great feeling from the beginning of the day slowly fades and is replaced by another... dread. But this time it feels different, as if I have a choice but what that choice is, is unclear. I watch the teacher across the hall as he closes his door. He has his hands in his pockets as he casually strolls down the crowded hall. He stops and chats with any student who makes eye contact.

My first class of the day has just ended, and already I am drained. I cannot figure out why I'm exhausted all the time. I am fit, run every day, but this doesn't translate into energy.

Later that day, I have a suicide disclosure. A student remains behind at the end of class. His first comment is, "I hate my life. I can't go on." He then simply puts his head down on the desk and lets it all out. I listen, and for twenty minutes he sobs. At one point I have to restrain him just to make him stop punching the desk.

How did his situation get this bad? I had not picked up a hint, body language, anything, to tell me he is this low. I am well into the school year, and I still don't know all their names. I see one hundred and ninety students every two days, not one of them do I know well.

The boy confides in me. I listen. I help. This should bring me satisfaction. It does not.

From the window of the education train, the summer's images are now a distorted painting, as if the speed of the train splashes water onto the canvas. Likewise, autumn's colors are fresher, yet they already begin to stream into one another. Losing the bottom line means losing ones' vision. I have lost the moment.

Chapter 8

I think that what we're seeking is an experience of being alive, so that our life experiences
on the purely physical plane will have reso-
nances within our own innermost being and
reality, so that we actually feel the rapture of
being alive.
~Joseph Campbell

As opening weeks mature into autumn months my depth of sadness and lack of energy for classes, even colleagues, becomes
appalling. It was once never, then sporadically, now it is an
everyday occurrence. The consistencies that took me to great
places in my teaching now simply mire me in a whirlwind of
deadlines. Yet, the only person who can impose some deadlines
is myself. Learning the student's names is my responsibility.
However, It's getting harder as so many come and go.

I give assignments for the sake of the percentage and
for the God called Curriculum. I despise marking to chart arbi-
trary progress. This was never why I became a teacher. The
mound of white paper on my desk is as faceless as the students
I teach. Students come and go, all the time wondering, "Why am
I here?" I find myself wondering the same thing. I used to have

such energy for this place. Has a calling simply turned into a "job?"

I am only partially into the school year, but am also early in my career. Already I'm sick of hearing the words "accountable" and "cooperative." They have no meaning, and—worse—no soul. They stifle thinking and serve only the bureaucracy.

Huxley's *Brave New World* taught of "free islands," places where conscious people live isolated from the rest of society. I once overheard my Scottish colleague explain that he "Tries to have an atmosphere in class of a civilized society." He called it "Cells of civilization." Huxley's "free islands" are comparable: a safe place where all had the right, even responsibility, "to think." I hope this still includes me.

I glance at the unmarked papers that form a barrier. They obscure not only my view of the empty desks but also the potential that so patiently still waits. It is now my turn to ask, "Why am I here?"

Maybe I was thinking out loud or maybe things are going on that I do not comprehend, but either way, a Scottish accent interrupts my thoughts. "Asking, 'why' is how consciousness finds the celestial shore of a 'free island.'"

I startle, almost knocking the pile of papers off my desk. "How do you know what I am thinking?"

He smiles, making his oft-broken nose point in several directions at once. "Isn't that really what we are all thinking, all the time?"

"You think people spend their time contemplating Huxley?"

He laughs heartily and shares. "No. They're asking 'why am I here?' all the time. Every waking moment. Most just aren't aware of it."

I stare at him with what I am sure is a ludicrous expression.

He softly asks, "Have you figured out yet, why schools have so many secretaries and so few counselors?"

I am embarrassed to admit that I have not given his question a second of thought.

He does not relent. "Have you asked yourself why you're a teacher, and what gives you the right?"

Something inside me breaks. "It's hard to find answers when the best you can do is survive."

He asks the question that I can not. "Is survival good enough?" I shake my head. "Excellent." He then studies me for a very long time as if he is deciding something monumental. Oddly, all he shares before leaving is, "We'll continue this conversation. Have a good evening."

I cannot honestly say that any of our brief conversations make me feel better. It is as if he knows something that I do not. In fact, I can definitely say that our encounters make me feel worse.

By the end of the day, I look like "Columbo" on a case—tired and worn. With the collar of my rain-jacket pulled up, I shuffle through puddles and squint as raindrops splash down. I throw my nightly load of homework into the jeep. My fellow teachers do the same. They look more like coal miners coming out of the mineshaft after their shift. Instead of blinking at the harsh daylight, they squint up at the streetlights that were on when they entered the building early that morning.

Some nights, my drive home is rewarding. I leave the city as quickly as possible. Soon cars are turning off, and the road becomes mine—not to speed but to luxuriate. On this section of the road I am away from the other stressed drivers, including the many that risk everything, everyday, to arrive home thirty seconds earlier —unconscious zombies, who grind gas pedals all for those thirty seconds. Once this madness is behind me, I become lost in self-indulgence. This is my time: a magical time of the in-between, when twilight and road become one, taking me from honorable work to trusted family.

The country roads that guide me home take odd twists and turns. The rural legend is that the individuals who built them liked certain flora, so the road bends for apparently no reason and the asphalt yields to a flower. There is something I like about that. I take my time and relax. Higher blood pressure and pounding heart are just not worth thirty seconds.

My mind wanders to how much money I earn. Another confrontation over contracts is brewing between government and teachers. Looking objectively at both sides, I see an argument where each side is often both wrong and right. This is the criterion for the human species: to become entrenched. Most of the debate, if it can be called that any longer, revolves around money. My brain calculates, and the results are surprising. If I just work nine to three, as some people mistakenly believe teachers do, I make an impressive and somewhat overpaid salary. If I calculate more accurately by including parent, student, and staff meetings, supervision, coaching, marking, extracurricular activities, clubs and other peripheral commitments, I actually make below minimum wage. Again, a salary that is undeserved. How could either side come to a fair solution?

My thoughts of money are depressing, so I choose to do something I love very much. I watch the clouds that form just off the coast—the watchers of history themselves, it has been said. In the city, and along the coast, they bring rain and darkness. I am envious of the little fishing boat that receives their blessing in the form of a drenching. I thrive in this setting. It drives me inward, and provides a cloak for my thoughts. I recall a poem written by Leonardo Da Vinci:

Every now and then go away,
have a little relaxation,
for when you come back
to your work
your judgment will be surer;
since to remain constantly at work
will cause you to lose power
Of judgment ...

Go some distance away
because the work appears smaller
and more of it
can be taken in at a glance,
and a lack of harmony
or proportion
is more readily seen.

Partially due to this poem, I pull over beside one of the many lakes that I drive past everyday. Stopping here after work, I always try to see what is here. It is my way of "Going some distance away." During this time, I never try to gaze or daydream. I simply concentrate to see what is really here. A loon echoes into the wilderness. Trees miraculously change the color of their leaves. Extra twigs have found their way into the eagle's nest. Beaver gnawings plug a side creek, and a new deer trail breaks from the tall grass. Nothing and everything.

Today, the weather has changed since I left work. The wind has picked up blowing away the zeppelin-like clouds.

Replacing them is a cold, crisp, fall day. The lake is bluer than I have ever seen. The sky is more azure than the lake. The trees show off too many colors to count. Impossible to ignore are the mountains with their startling white peaks. Surrounded by all this beauty, in my mind's eye I see my family. They belong in this scene. I have so much, yet something is siphoning this consciousness from me.

I pull into my garage again feeling as if my life force is patiently draining away.

Chapter 9

What a wonderful life I've had! I only wish I'd realized it sooner.
~Collette

My role as an educator is to be the best human being I can. Same in my role as parent, husband and friend, but sometimes it is so easy to deviate from that responsibility. When this happens, I feel like a hypocrite—and quickly become regular, routine, and part of the problem. It is so easy to lose purpose. H. G. Wells once said. "More and more, human history is a race between education and catastrophe." I am not sure that I am winning.

After closing the garage door, I feel thankful for finally being home. It has always struck me as powerful how perspective plays such a role in our life.

For the rest of the night, I put the perfect combination of cedar, fir, and pine in the fireplace and watch it burn. No television, radio, or reading: just my family and a fire. There is perfect solitude here, perfect peace. Even Lab does not want to go outside for his nightly romp with the smells. I contemplate having my family near, children safe in bed, wife I love so much sleeping curled beside me. Just like when I was by the lake, I come to a realization that I have so much.

Sitting in front of the fire, despite the snoring dog, my mind finds itself searching through the school hallways. I did not realize the degree that I am putting up walls and closing doors. The more I acknowledge that the school's pace is not only busy but also sad, the more my walls rise in the name of survival.

As my mind drifts, rain pings off the metal roof. I see myself everyday less as a person and disappointingly more as an automaton. This makes my mood in tune with the school—sad. How can I become the teacher I want to be, if I cannot evolve into the person I should be? A Scottish accented voice echoes in my mind. *"Why are you a teacher?"* This is followed by another echo. *"What gives you the right?"* A strange realization comes over me—I feel more like a product of society than of substance, something created by the culture and not who I can be.

A cedar branch gathered from the last storm releases a loud crack as it burns in the fireplace. I look up in time to see the hot red sparks dripping down on the rest of the fire. It is as if a note, frozen secretly in the wood, is finally called upon to sing long after wind song has moved on. This sight and sound makes me think of falling leaves. In turn that makes me think not of the beautiful day but, oddly, of children—children falling out of school. I see their sad faces as the educational train speeds successfully to its destination.

Eventually, my wife and I decide to go up to our loft. First however, we give Lab his favorite chew toy and then look in on our children. I have so much!

Chapter 10

We cannot live only for ourselves. A thousand
fibers connect us with our fellow men; and
along those fibers, as sympathetic threads, our
actions run as causes, and they come back to
us as effects.
~Herman Melville

First thing upon waking is to get a fire started before my family is up. I have it down to a fine art—cedar kindling combined with less pine. Once I hear crackling and see red coals it is time for a larger piece of cedar, for both heat and sound—then bigger pieces of fir and pine for substance, and more cedar to lightly season the sputtering flames. I always try for the perfect fire. It's all about quality.

I enjoy being the first up and warming the house. It is something that my Dad did for our family and I hope my sons do for theirs. As I gaze into the fire, I wonder if that is what I am feeling at work. Is it about quality, about believing in something?

While I'm rubbing my hands to get the chill off, the loft is getting toasty. Three kids sneak past, and giggle upstairs to join my wife. That makes me feel good. I make an effort every morning to show my love for my wife and kids. It's the only way to start a day.

It turned cold during the night, and I have to scrape frost from my jeep for the first time this year. It labors getting started, but eventually we angle down the driveway. I take the usual route to work. This means going past the same three lakes from last night. As the previous night, I stop to look. At the shore I remember how this tradition began. My father and I did this when I was a child.

Dad would stop the car on the way to school and out we would jump. "Look up," he'd say. A flock of geese flew overhead. "Now, close your eyes. Can you hear them?" I can never see flocks without closing my eyes and thinking of him. One time, we walked across a damp field towards a cow. As any ten year old would, I asked, "Why are we doing this?" Dad's answer was, "So that my son will grow up knowing this sound. It's the most contented sound in the world." Even as I stand by this lakeshore, I can close my eyes and hear a cow chewing.

On yet another excursion, he stopped the car and I could not figure out what it was that he wanted me to see. In confusion, I clambered out and joined him. We both stared at a different kind of fence. It was ten feet high and had vicious, jagged metal on top. Despite my being just a child, Dad was showing me a prison. Looking through the fence, we could see the four-foot thick walls. Dad bent down and whispered. "I'd die if I had to spend even one day in there." I will make sure that I too stop, so my kids hear the sound of a loon and see the eyes of a wolf, as well as the absolute walls of a prison.

The sun is just coming up over the snow-capped eternal mountains. The wind streaming down brings high country air and the smell of fresh snow. The leaves have changed even within the last twelve hours. Frost and strong winds spill leaves to the ground where they freeze, as if they have twin anchors, one called dread and the other guilt.

This stop, as always, takes only a moment. Maybe it is just a simple rebellious act, an act of defiance aiming at all the drivers who try to gain those thirty seconds on the way home. I give up two, three, even occasionally a frivolous four minutes to stop and see. These moments are when I am most alive.

I turn to climb back into my jeep when I step on a frozen leaf. The crunch! I can still hear Dad say, "Hear that?" Instead of getting back into the jeep, I walk to a sheet of ice covering a tiny puddle. I tap it with my toe the way children do and listen to the ice crack. Thanks, Dad!

The heater in my jeep blasts away as I continue on. These moments give me energy. I recall a children's novelist who once said, "A child experiences an entire universe in a raindrop, on a window pain, one Tuesday afternoon." Driving to work with energy is much like sleeping well, a good run, or a hot shower—absolutely revitalizing. This day has the potential to be magical.

The roads in the city are icy, and that, of course, makes the zombies drive ten miles an hour faster. I arrive in the parking lot and, as I have grown to expect, the custodian is already out salting. After parking, I sprint towards a sheet of ice and lock my legs sliding across it. While I skim past a small group of students, they turn and watch. They all have odd expressions as if to say, "What's he on?" That's okay. At least they notice me. By the entrance, a student slips and falls. He is unhurt but ten dollars falls out of his pocket. In his embarrassment, he does not notice. I pick it up and call to him. "You dropped this." Turning, he snatches the money and, without so much as a "Thank you," continues into the school. No acknowledgement whatsoever. Am I turning invisible already? "You're welcome," I mumble to no one.

The crowded halls have the smell of wet jackets. There are also a surprising number of students who are too cool for jackets. They are easy to identify—skinny purple arms, wet t-shirts, and a cough of which any life-addicted smoker would be ashamed. How do their parents allow them to leave home dressed like that?

So far, the day has been good. It's a motivating day, reminding me why teaching is my career choice.

Sadly, two incidents detract from the satisfaction. Fourth period begins with a counselor telling me that one of my students has been the victim of a failed abduction early this morning. It has been on the noon news, so she wants me to talk to the class about it. My effort to explain how catastrophic this event might have been meets sheer boredom and shoulder shrugs.

The other incident involves a new student registering in my class. His previous teacher removed him for setting his book on fire. He sits with his back to me and through body language tells me to, "Take a hike." The highlight of class is the lack of smoke coming from his desk. Every time I try to help, he mumbles, "Whatever." I translate this to mean. "Leave me alone. Can't you see I'm irrelevant?"

Into my class he finds himself dumped, no consultation, just appearing, neither he nor I part of the process. Truth is, there is no process, just a reactive decision. This train is driven by the expedient decision. Move on, another crises will be here soon enough.

It is a no-win situation. If he leaves, I am another reminder that he is not important. If he stays, how does he get the help his actions cry out for? With his attitude, I cannot watch him every moment and teach. The best solution I can think of is for him to do his studying at the office. This allows me to teach the other students while the administration has to acknowledge his acting out. I cannot perceive any other way for him to get access to the services that he deserves and support he needs. I am genuinely doing this to help him.

Unfortunately, the look he gives me says it all. I catch myself with an expression that agrees. It's okay kid; I feel irrelevant as well.

Driving to school today I felt on the brink of something great, something magical and something no one could take away. By the end of the day, that feeling is gone.

These experiences, these thoughts rock me. I am trying to be a great teacher, but sometimes I simply feel abandoned.

On the way home, I pull over where I stopped this morning. This place seems to beckon, as if a lesson waits. My little puddle still has the ice shards from where I stepped. A reminder of better times. I am a little later than yesterday, so most of the trees and lake are in darkness. Only the peaks of the majestic mountains continue reflecting a purple-pink sunset. The wind is blowing hard now. The winds of change. Winter is coming.

I love the days when I see both sunrise and sunset. Even days like this, that begin so full of promise and end like a dinosaur stuck in a tar pit. The more he struggles the worse it gets. Nevertheless, struggle he must. I look for the frozen leaf but it has discarded its anchors, dread and guilt, and blown on down the road.

Chapter 11

The most beautiful thing we can experience is the mysterious. It is the source of all true art and all science. He to whom this emotion is a stranger, who can no longer pause to wonder and stand rapt in awe, is as good as dead: his eyes are closed.
~Albert Einstein

One thing that always gives me energy is the weekend. I try to work out six days a week. Never, however, on Friday. Friday is to meet friends for a drink, or arrive home early and do something special with my kids. By not working out, it seems like every weekend is a long weekend. This also gives me more energy for my Saturday run. If I ever experience bliss in my life, it might well be during my early morning run. Twelve miles total, past three lakes, then a sharp right along a trail straight up into the mountains. Then eventually down a small valley and up along a ridge to two other lakes and finally the road home. At the end, I walk my driveway to cool down while Lab swaggers out to greet me. I finish by sitting on the balcony looking at the view, dripping sweat and drinking water. It is here that my sense of oneness is most defined.

The wind has been building for days, until this Saturday morning when it finally lets loose. The rain is coming down sideways, and it is only experience that gets me out the door, knowing that, once wet, I will get used to it and eventually even enjoy it. An added bonus is to know that when my run is complete the mystical shower waits. I finish stretching, kiss my wife and yell goodbye to the kids in the loft. I look for Lab, who is hiding. It is after all, raining.

By the end of the driveway I am soaked, happy, and ready to go. The first view of the lake is only fifty yards from the driveway, at the top of a small rise. This is the best perspective to see the lake for the first time. As I jog up the slight incline the lake is actually above me, and soon I am beside it. Just stunning. The road begins flat and binds itself to the lakeshore. It then meanders up and down, left and right, past two more lakes. I take a sharp right up a well-used deer trail and here my climb begins. It will take thirty-three minutes until the trail flattens. It is good to be in the trees, as the rainforest offers protection. I can hear wind-song again, and with the help of treetops it tunes up. I can almost close my eyes and run this trail. This allows me to focus on my pace and not the ankle-twisting roots.

Running up mountains has taught me many things about honesty, patience, commitment, and trust. Honesty, because you cannot lie to yourself; if you are not in shape, you cannot fake it half way up. Patience, because if you go too fast you are going to be in a whole world of pain. You learn early in your mountain-running career that patience really is a virtue. Commitment, because there is literally no way of getting up a mountain without it. Finally trust—once you are at the top, no matter how tired you are, you must trust your conditioning to get you back. There is a great amount of consciousness in trusting yourself.

A third of the way up the trail, another factor comes into play. The temperature is dropping and it will affect my rhythm. This does not concern me, as I have learned to run with just enough effort to stay warm. Too slow and you cannot maintain body heat; too fast and you will overheat, losing your ability to fight off the cold. The path I follow bends at the summit, drops into a valley and then follows a ridge.

Soon, I look down into the small harbor my wife and I chose to make our home. It is as pacific a scene as any human on the planet will ever see. Small boats dot the harbor, the odd one leaving a silver path as it cuts through the blue. I always experience a runner's high at this point. This makes me light as I look down on my life and my log home. Down there, at times, I act and feel as if I am afraid of my own shadow. Up here, on this trail, my lightness makes me think I have no shadow. I am more conscious here.

Suddenly, I notice snowflakes. The first flakes of the year always seem so large. Every year, the first snowfall I see is usually on this trail and it is always spiritual. In my solitude, I yell out, "Bon Hiver!" The universe answers; it comes in the form of the here and now.

The flakes start to float down in serious numbers. They drift in absolute silence. The trail drops slightly and the wind stops. I slow my stride to enjoy the spectacle. In these conditions there is a surreal, almost three-dimensional effect while running. I wish I could run here forever. The sense of peace is overwhelming.

My pace slows slightly as I continue along the ridge. For some unknown reason I think of my student. Penny! It is extraordinary, but while I run I recall a conversation overheard between her and a teacher the previous day. Very strange that I should remember a discussion to which I thought I had paid no attention. The two of them were talking in the hallway as

I unconsciously passed. Somehow, up here, I remember every word.

Penny is explaining to her teacher. "One reason I don't talk much in class is because words are very sacred. Words are like stones. People carry the words that others give them. In your pockets, little pebbles in your ears, as well as big boulders in your socks, stones everywhere, all sizes and shapes. You become very heavy and tire easily. It's hard to move, and you soon lose the ability to fly. A person must be light so that they can fly to their dreams."

The teacher asks, "So you're saying that one's words have an impact?"

Penny responds. "Words have weight. You can place some by the side of the road so you can fly, or let others anchor you to the ground so you can't move. You may also keep only chosen ones, so you have balance. These stones help guide you. You can use them to build bridges or walls. The stones you choose to keep, throw away, or pass on, impact the weight of yourself and others."

The teacher then adds. "This would mean that you and your words exist. Interesting."

Penny responds with pure humility. "Yes."

Unfortunately, I could not recall who the teacher was.

For a brief shining moment, I have an epiphany. It lasts but a moment and then is gone, but the effect will last my lifetime. I stop running and for no apparent reason start to cry. I sob like the student who told me he could not go on, and "hated life." I actually fall onto my knees—or more accurately, my legs buckle.

Beside me I see my shadow, also on its knees. Its tears look like river rocks tumbling over each other as they submit to gravity and rain to the ground. I watch in amazement while small piles of stones begin to form at my feet. As the great slide of pebbles, rocks, and boulders fall, my shadow loses definition. It is as if every word, every syllable, ever said to me is being examined. Suddenly, my twin anchors of dread and guilt simply blow on down the road.

I feel lighter, and ideas clarify. I recall how the conversation ends between teacher and student. I can finally see that the teacher is my Scottish colleague. He says to Penny, "Thanks for sharing this with me. Now I understand a little better why you are so quiet. It must be hard for you, with me always asking you to speak up in class."

She answers. "Yes."

The teacher ends by saying, "Once again, I've learned so much from you today. Thanks, Penny."

The only stone she lays at his feet is one small pebble. "Yes."

My epiphany is simple. I have never seen a teacher learn from a student before. Yet for them, it appears to be an everyday conversation.

I lope up the driveway, and only then realize that my run is over. Somehow, I had gotten off my knees and continued. I ran with so many thoughts, simultaneously leaving my own rocks along the way, which allows me to feel even lighter. I wonder if this is why I always enjoy running in the mountains—the place the biggest rocks call home.

I cool down along the driveway as Lab greets me from the safety of his dog door. His wobbling head reveals that his tail is wagging a hello. I cannot expect him to come out, since it is still raining. From their favorite place on rainy days, the kids yell out the loft window, "Snowing in the mountains?"

"Sure is," I answer while realizing the bill of my cap still carries snow. As I enter the house I notice that a few flakes are determined enough to make it all the way down to the lakes. Inside, Lab greets me, standing on his back legs, while front paws flail about searching for a hug. I sense no embarrassment in him. I assume he carries very few rocks.

Velcro rips as I strip off layers of clothing. Steam dutifully fogs over the bathroom with warmth. Stepping into the shower is again euphoric. Relaxing in the warm spray, I think back to my run. I wonder when was the last time a student taught me anything. Had my ego become so big that I was no longer able to *stand under* another person in order to *understand?* I suddenly realize that to evolve, my ego must be less. There is the true lesson of my epiphany!

While hot water takes away the cold and effort, I think of what has happened during my run. My first epiphany is small, and happens far away in the mountains. My ego has been too big. When Penny said, "Yes," in response to that teacher for the third time, she said it with such wisdom. It is the type of wisdom born out of much pain.

Stepping out of the shower, I have the oddest thought. In two weeks, it will be December 21st. The first day of winter, the shortest day of the year, the day when my "shadow," exists the least amount of time. Would this provide an opportunity to lose part of my ego? I am immediately aware of something that I have almost forgotten. The education train that left the station to start the school year had ignored a little girl. She had been crying. As with me, stones fell from her eyes and built a wall around her. I realize that little girl was Penny.

Deep pain caused her tears. Those stones that piled at her feet were making room for wisdom. They had been forming a wall around her. Was the first glimpse of consciousness actually building walls to survive? Did those tears mean a small ego, and would that give me room for wisdom? I have earned the knowledge, that by answering these questions, the compensation is not just an understanding of survival. It is an awareness of consciousness and all that it entails.

Walking gingerly downstairs, stiff from the run, I am content that only my corporeal body is suffering while my spirit soars.

Chapter 12

When you are inspired by some great purpose, some extraordinary project all your thoughts break their bonds; Your mind transcends limitations, your consciousness expands in every direction, and you find yourself in a new, great and wonderful world. Dormant forces, faculties and talents become alive, and you discover yourself to be a greater person by far than you ever dreamed yourself to be.
~Patanjali

From my classroom window, I stare at the familiar mountain range far in the distance. My students perspire over an exam, and I notice Penny biting her pencil, anticipating a catastrophe. Behind the failure, maybe there really is a great kid. What can I do to earn the privilege of seeing that? The questions, *"Why are you a teacher, and what gives you the right?"* pound in my brain.

Across the hall is the teacher who placed these questions inside me. He always seems to have a huge amount of fun at work. His class often distracts mine with their laughter. My students finish their exam papers and glumly stack them on my desk. I notice Penny does not make eye contact as she places her half-finished test on the growing pile.

Left alone for a whole four minutes between classes I sit at the front of my room. The uncluttered desk of that first week, and much of the potential, is now a long-forgotten memory. I look sideways and glare at my marking. I know which students will fail without so much as a glance at the tests. The mound of paper has grown high enough to obscure my view of the mountain range. I try to gather energy for the next class. The students are already piling in.

I notice the trees in the park sway with the rhythm of the breeze. Instead of restoring my energy, it wraps a veil of survival around me. This is what being immune feels like. Even the slight breeze reminds me of the education train. Just like the wind, the train never stops. Occasionally a new passenger grabs on, but more often one falls off.

Where along this journey did I become immune? Furthermore, from what am I immune? Thirty-five more passengers sit waiting.

Despite my concerns, it is a good class. One student who rarely participates got into a debate with an "A" student. He holds his own and he knows it. I think he surprised himself, and that makes us both proud. These are the moments that teaching is all about.

This sadly balances an incident at the end of class. An unkind word by one student motivates another to react: a torn-up worksheet, and then an exchange of words. I try speaking to the offender but no one is listening. My class waits and I consider sending him to the office but instead ask a counselor to help. I hope a consequence or apology will be appropriate, or at the very least understanding. Instead, after five minutes he swaggers back into class without even knocking on the door.

He has told the counselor that it wouldn't happen again, and so the incident is closed. As the momentum of the train propels us forward, no lesson is learned. Expediency rules. We all just pick up where we left off. Nothing changes. We cannot slow the train even to teach a lesson! What really hurts is that everyone accepts this. Counselor, student, even me, we all become unconscious for the sake of the almighty train.

At the end of the day, I talk with the offending student. This confirms my worst fears. The lesson of remorse or at the very least responsibility is non-existent. I think no consequence, no lesson. Deep down I think: no pain, no wisdom.

I leave my class sad and tired. Why am I robbed of the energy that the day promised? Instead of traveling home, I have a staff meeting to attend. Although everybody is pressed for time, I still find it rude to mark during meetings—but the train's schedule does not allow for respect. I listen while a debate about grading behavior heats up. Some staff want to grade behavior while others are concerned that some would use it punitively. One individual mentions that it isn't school policy. I chuckle thinking that she would make a good engineer on a train.

In most meetings I rarely speak. I have seen too many take up others' time just to massage their ego. This time however, I speak. "If we do not have time to deal with student's behavior, possibly a mark will have an effect."

Would the train slow to deal with behavior? Only time will tell if I have any impact.

Walking out of the meeting, two teachers approach, and one asks me. "How do you do it?"

"Do what?" I query.

"In these staff meetings, when they ask you to do thirty-six things and you only have time to do eleven, how do you do it?" It was a rhetorical question and we laugh... sadly.

His question makes me think how every new conductor asks the train to go faster, all in the name of efficiency. The other teacher who has joined us is my Scottish colleague, and he says, "I thought I was the stir stick on staff." I throw my nightly marking into the back seat. He adds something that clarifies the entire day; "If nothing changes, nothing changes." It is my turn to stare at him. He has just summed up everything I feel.

He then makes a most profound comment. "Be careful about spending too much time on the students' behavior." I look at him quizzically because this is odd coming from someone that I perceive to be the consummate professional. He enlightens. "The more time you spend on behavior the less influence you will have. Don't ever ignore behavior, but the more time you spend building a relationship with a student, the more influence you will have on their behavior."

As I sit in traffic waiting for the light, I grasp what he is saying. If I spend my energy dealing only with my students' behavior I will lose my relationship with them. However, if I build bridges I gain influence.

As the light changes I hit the gas, and a most peculiar thought floats through my consciousness. Would I ever have the energy to write a book? I doubt it.

My stop on the way home tonight is brief because the end-of-autumn winds have turned cold. The snow line is dropping as it obeys nature.

Within moments of dumping my load of marking on the kitchen table, I have a perfect fire warming the house. I so want to hurl my marking into the flames. Oops, sorry kids, I tripped, you all have to redo the work.

The wind outside is starting to whine, a prelude to louder tunes. The treetops begin their dance. It's going to be a wind-song night. This raises my spirit.

It is also board-game night. I love this time with my family. The kids will never be too old for this stuff. Girlfriends and boyfriends will never be their priority. Well... at least for tonight the board game is their whole world. We play while our little log home protects us from the wind. Suddenly, we sit quietly and grimace as wind-song bullies its way through the trees and takes a fierce run at our home. It is comforting to know that Lab is safe inside. The candles are already lit in preparation of the coming power failure.

I toss another log on the fire as our game heats up. When the room fills with warmth, my children's eyes eventually droop, so we carry them to bed. I want to reflect on the last few days, so I explain that I am attending the fire. My wife kindly offers to stay, but I tell her it is unnecessary as I have much to ponder.

Running in the mountains, I had an epiphany that allows me to see myself from a different perspective. Sitting by myself, I notice the light of the flames casting my shadow on the wall. It is haunting to realize that only I stand between my perfect fire and my imperfect shadow. I think of my Scottish friend and remember him saying, "Sometimes I wonder where my shadow is. But then I wait and it usually catches up." His reference to his "shadow" was confusing but I am beginning to understand.

When the wind rests, catching its breath, quiet rules. During this time, it is as if I am almost able to hear myself. Is wisdom really born only out of pain? Surely that is not the only way to learn. I look at my own life and know, when forced upon me, only then are my deepest lessons learned. Possibly that is just part of the human condition, making our species slow learners indeed. The wind builds again and my hand absent-mindedly drops to stroke Lab behind his ears. He lets out a yawn and a sigh, so content that any human would be envious.

As predicted, the lights flick out as a tree comes down

somewhere along the road. The candles allow me to go around and shut off the light switches so they will not wake anyone when they come back on. Sitting down, I pull my chair close to the fire. In the silence between the waves of wind, only disturbed by an occasional, "crack" from the firewood, I feel a cosmic hug and peace of mind. It is as if life itself whispers to me, "You are doing fine, just keep going." Then this moment is broken by a shriek of wind. I look once more at my shadow on the wall and chuckle, wondering how it feels about the coming of the shortest day of the year.

My epiphany had allowed me to realize that my shadow and I are one and the same. I have earned the right to see my angst. I did not know that it would be only my first epiphany, and that there was more to come.

I do not remember how I finished my run that day, but I realize that if I had stayed there long, my rocks would have built a wall around me that I could never tear down. With this first step of consciousness comes the caveat that if I do not lose ego, the walls will remain forever. While running, my epiphany dropped rocks along the way, making my ego smaller. To survive, I will always need to remain safe behind my wall, my ego. To live however, I will have to evolve and transcend my wall; I will have to lose my "Shadow." I need to become conscious, and my ego must make room for evolution. This will allow for consciousness, which in turn teaches me the lesson of paradox. I need those walls to survive, but to live, I will have to tear them down. This is my first experience in the world of choice! A land between "Shadow" and "Substance"—this is the paradox—for part of me to grow, part of me must die.

Substance: The main content, the essential, underlying reality of something in which accidents, qualities, attributes and phenomena occur, the real main or important part of anything.

It is wisdom to know others,
It is enlightenment to know one's self.
~Lao Tsu

Chapter 13

If you wish to glimpse inside a human soul and
get to know a man ... just watch him laugh. If
he laughs well, he's a good man.
~Fyodor Dostoyevsky

A few days pass, and I spend far too much time wrapped in
the security of my shadow. However, it is empowering to realize that for the first time I am at least aware of this. Today
is December twenty-first, the shortest day of the year. Driving
to work, I am sure the day will fly, as it is also the last day of
classes before Christmas holidays.

Unfortunately, time does not cooperate; it procrastinates,
drags, and dawdles, doing anything but fly.

It is a day like any other, just slower. The students are understandably excited and the staff undeniably exhausted. Staff
and students alike just want to go home and start holidays. I
do not have the energy or enthusiasm to stay for the staff gift
exchange, and leave feeling heavy. While driving away, I look
at the school in my rear view mirror. Befitting my mood, a black
cloud hangs over the building. It appears to wait for the final
good-byes before releasing rain on everyone dashing for their
cars. Staring deep within its form, I detect a smirk.

Yet another day began with optimism and potential, but ends with nothing. One small ray of hope comes, oddly, in the form of an immense weather system rolling over the mountains. It is getting colder, and I can tell that the roads will be icy in just a few hours. Rain begins in earnest and I pull over to observe the gigantic weather front. Massive clouds stride over the mountains like a cotton colossus. Nothing but this weather system can dwarf the jagged range that stretches across the horizon. It makes me feel small, and therefore my problems shrink. I feel as alive as I have all day.

Driving, I have a sad sense of vindication. The dark cloud over the school is insignificant, and pales next to the rolling thunder that flashes and crashes over an entire mountain range.

When I finally arrive at the end of the driveway, Lab frantically dashes out to share all the day's events with me. One of the peculiarities of this rather peculiar dog is that wherever he goes he carries his food bowl in his mouth. No one has ever taught him this, but my kids attribute it to the Boy Scout in him. "Always be prepared," as one never knows when food might arrive. At this point in our greeting ritual, he usually does me the honor of dropping his bowl and taking my hand to guide me around the yard. It is his way of showing me what happened during his day.

However, just before he is able to do this, there is a bright light followed by an ear-splitting crack of thunder. I am nearly hit in the head, not by the lightening, but by Lab's bowl as it flies into the air. In the millisecond it takes me to realize what is happening, a tail disappears through the dog door. I run after him as cold wet drops begin to splatter the ground. Inside, whimpering comes from a dog that has no bowl. My consoling does no good as he paces.

Despite the thunder, his courage wins the day, and I have never been so proud of him. I open the door and at warp speed he races out, ears pinned back, crying in fear during the entire frantic dash. Without breaking stride he scoops up his bowl and, trying to bleed off speed, forces his head to aim toward the house while his back legs skid out from under him. This makes his circle route as small as the laws of physics allow. I open the door just slightly wider than his terror-filled eyes. Focusing on his destination with one mighty leap through the opening, he slides across the floor and with a loud grunt bashes into the wall on the other side of the room. With his bowl tightly gripped in canine teeth, he has made it! A finer display of courage I have never seen.

I congratulate and then console him, as thunder shatters our moment. We share unimaginable trust as he allows me to pry the just saved bowl from his jaws and place it beside his blanket. Still panting, he sprawls next to it. I lie beside him and pat his head, muttering, "Good boy. Good dog." Despite the thunder, we are both thankful: he for his bowl and me for my dog.

Today is the same as so many other days—eventful, yet somehow I can intuitively feel I have not experienced all that it offered. What would the day have brought if I had the same courage as my dog?

While I help my wife prepare dinner, our children play upstairs. Their volume reveals that they have plenty of pent-up energy in anticipation of the coming holidays. If it continues to rain, we will all soon have cabin fever. My daughter must have read my mind as I hear her on the telephone with the neighbors, making sure our traditional visit to their ranch is organized.

At dinner, I gather some candles. Once they're lit, I turn off the dining-room lights. My two sons chide, "How romantic," while my wife and daughter watch curiously. Wanting to surprise everyone by revealing that the thunderstorm had been replaced by gently falling snow, I walk over to the outdoor light switch and simultaneously flick it on and shout, "Look!" Four heads look but five voices gasp. I had not realized that a family of deer was standing just outside our dining-room window. Our collective gasp causes them to raise their heads. None of us can contain our joy.

Our excitement does not abate as we discuss tomorrow. We will all walk the mile-and-change of combined country back roads and trails to our neighbors. Along the way, we will pick the family Christmas tree and make plans for the next two weeks. Upon arrival, we will immediately go to the back porch to toast the season by popping a bottle of champagne, aiming the cork into the back yard. When the season turns to spring, we will look for it—at which time we traditionally sacrifice another bottle. If it is just light rain or a nice day, the kids will spend it horseback riding. They, of course, wish for snow so they can go for their traditional sleigh-ride while my wife and I will stroll to a quaint neighborhood pub. It's a wonderful way to begin our holiday.

After dinner, we all sit bundled on our covered balcony with the house lights off, and discuss all that tomorrow might bring. It is snowing heavily now, so the possibility of a sleigh-ride is excellent. I ask my wife, "How long have you known our neighbors? You knew them before we met."

"I knew Marco when we were both just kids," she explains, "The entire family has been near and dear to my heart, and they've influenced me, well, forever. I can always count on them at a moment's notice. Through my whole life, they've been a source of laughter and goodwill. Whenever I question my life, their level of love and caring reminds me what a family is supposed to be."

My oldest son asks, "How did they do that?"

"Good question. They always kept their word, while raising the spirits of others by sharing a laugh. I never thought of it before, but they make themselves a family through laughter. Fridays they'd invite me over for dinner, and we would just sit around, content. I used to look forward to that so much."

Our children listen as if they are looking into a secret adult world. I like that. My wife continues, "I remember Marco's father lost his arm in a mill accident, but amazingly worked for the same company for another forty years. Throughout all my memories, from childhood to this very moment, I can hear his laugh. What an amazing family! Their doors were always open, and out into the neighborhood their laughter would spill. When he told one of his jokes, most of the time he never got to the punchline because he was laughing so hard. No one ever minded; you would just get caught up in the moment and find yourself laughing along." As she shares, I notice a far-away look in her eyes.

"I recall sitting at their little kitchen table, talking, while their canaries interrupted us with song. Food would come and go, as did visitors, but the constants were always the open door and the laughter. Marco's father always asked me to call him by his first name, but out of true respect, I never did. He loved making fortified red wine, and I vividly remember the time I walked down the back alley to their house and saw fifteen cats rolling on their backs while another five napped. A red fluid dripped from under his garage door then ran down the lane. I thought something terrible had happened but when I heard his belly-laugh, I knew everything was okay. His 'still' had broken, and the leaked red wine was being enjoyed by all the felines in the neighborhood."

Her far-away look is gone now, as I watch her pick up our daughter and place her on her lap. "I was so lucky to have them in my life. When he saw those cats, he laughed so hard. That belly-laugh of his carried me through many dark moments. That family taught me that if I fall; all I have to do is open these wings called laughter. I can always choose to float to a better place."

My wife's soft voice, the quiet of the evening and the attentive audience make for a wonderful night of storytelling. I particularly cherish these evenings, because our children receive a deeper picture of where we come from, and that in turn helps them know themselves. I look out into the yard at the snow blanketing the ground, and realize I have only seen my shadow once today.

I suggest it is bedtime, and the kids gather all their remaining energy for one last effort. "One more story."

"Yeah, tell us one of your friend's stories that made you laugh."

"Yeah please, one story."

There was the predictable collective, "Please!"

I look at my wife, knowing what her answer will be.

"Okay, but just one. You have to remember most of his stories never really end. He always laughed at his own stories, then we would all giggle, and that was how they ended."

"Did he ever finish one?" they ask in unison.

"Come to think of it, I do remember one about a dog." Mom winks in my direction, knowing how much they love dog stories. It is pure coincidence that Lab wanders over and, with a tail-wag, plops down. "He told me this story when I was about your age. In the basement of their house there's a laundry-room where they have the usual stuff: washer, dryer, towels—you know, stuff. He is down there by himself doing laundry when Bodie, everyone's favorite neighborhood dog, comes to visit. Bodie ran the neighborhood, and often walked into people's homes to see what was up. Now, you have to understand, he was a great dog but he had one bad habit. Bodie was a thief. He'd steal single shoes, rags, things a dog wants. He never damaged anything. He just took them to his bed for company, or attention, or for reasons only a dog understands.

Well, it was laundry time, so when Bodie wanders into the room, their dad closes the sliding door so that he doesn't have to stop the dog if he steals anything. Then their dad makes the mistake of not paying much attention to him. So naturally, Bodie tries to steal something. Dad sees him out of the corner of his eye trying to abscond with a freshly cleaned shirt, and so he yells, 'Drop it!'

Startled, poor Bodie turns to escape and accidentally pulls a towel down on top of himself, covering his head. Panicking and now blind, he runs head-first into the closed door, breaking it and knocking himself out. So their dad is standing over a dog that's now lying on the floor, unconscious, covered in a towel. Poor Bodie's four exposed legs are splayed in four different directions.

His wife hears the crash and runs downstairs to see a broken door. Once she forces the splinters open, the scene she sees is her husband, who's probably the gentlest person in the world, standing over an apparently dead dog with a towel respectfully covering it. 'Bodie's dead!' his wife screams, 'What did you do to him?' Her husband answers slightly confused, 'I just yelled for him to drop it.' Well, husband and wife stand there staring at each other, not sure what to do next.

Then, Bodie makes a miraculous recovery. With the towel still on his head, he stands and staggers between the two astonished humans. Mom lets out a scream because she thought the poor dog was dead. "It's a miracle!" she yells. Of course, Dad thinks this is hilarious. Poor Bodie wobbles on four wonky legs through the shattered door, and after about ten feet he shakes, dropping the towel to the floor. Mom mutters, 'It's a bloody miracle,' while Dad is laughing so hard, he couldn't make it to the top of the stairs without sitting for a moment. Bodie leaves the house vaguely recognizing the street leading to his home. He then attempts to save his pride with one final indignant glance back at the two people who now stand on the front lawn doubled over in laughter."

As the story ends, I think what good laughs my kids have, vibrant and from their hearts. My backyard has turned into a winter wonderland as the kids and Mom keep their word and decide it is bedtime.

Lab and I sit in front of the fireplace with logs crackling. At my feet Lab dreams of tomorrow's activities, and I gaze out over the harbor. My country log home literally wraps itself around me. During the night, it continues to snow and I wonder about those eternal questions: who am I, and what do I believe in?

Chapter 14

All man's miseries derive from not being able
to sit quietly in a room alone.
~Blaise Pascal

Is there a quieter time than the first serious snowfall of the
year? Possibly the next morning, when first you sense it, then
pull back the curtains verifying what you somehow already
know. A foot of white insulation covers the ground.

Such is the case at dawn. Moments after rising I pose
the question: "Should I start a fire or do you want to go for a
hike?" In unison the kids yell, "Sleigh-ride! Sleigh-ride!" In
record time, with Lab leading the way, our journey begins. This
daylong adventure is our family's version of a walk-about. We
have a destination in mind, but between here and there we will
meander wherever our interests please.

The previous night's snowfall shows no sign of letting
up, which means this trek will be slowed by snow angels and
snowball fights. Lab tries to be included, but quickly becomes
distracted by the smell of a rabbit or the screech of a hawk.
Adventure and fun fill the two-kilometer hike. Along the way,
our kids traditionally pick the family Christmas tree that I mark
and later cut. Their criteria for the chosen tree always eludes

me—one year a sixteen-foot fir, the next year a scrawny two-foot pine. Every year I ask, "What type of tree this year?" Their response is always the same. "We'll know when we see it."

We have almost finished our trip when the kids follow Lab off the trail. Shouts of "We found it!" break the silence. Holding hands with my wife, I stroll over to find them standing beside this year's choice. It is a cute, perfectly cone-shaped, four-foot high spruce. I have no idea why, out of the thousands of trees we passed, they chose this one. I dutifully mark it, and one night soon will come back on my own and drag it home.

The last section of our hike is my favorite. The trail stops at a small hillock that overlooks our neighbor's ranch. We observe smoke billowing from their chimney, as friendly a sight on a winter's day as anything that our pioneering ancestors cherished. Our friends are already trudging up the hill, dragging something behind them as they come to greet us. The kids and Lab take off to help. There is movement down by the barn as the neighbor's grandkids hitch up horses to a magnificent sleigh.

Our children tramp back to us, and when they get close I see what they are now dragging. "Perfect," I whisper to my wife. We thank our old friends for the gifts. Our kids now have antique 'Snow Rocket' sleds, and we of course ask, "Can old Mom and Dad use them to get down the hill?" Their response is giggling, and then all we see are the soles of their feet as they belly flop onto the sleds and rocket down the hill. By the time we reach the bottom, they have been up and down five times, and poor Lab is sitting, tongue hanging out, fed up with that game.

We do our traditional champagne toast and then, drawn by two huge, beautiful, black horses, the sleigh arrives in the backyard. We lift our kids onto the blankets beside our friends and make plans to return in the late afternoon. With hot chocolate in hand, along with small Swiss bells jingling, they go off on a grand adventure. Loyal Lab trots in the lead, barking directions. My wife and I wave as they vanish behind a curtain of falling snowflakes. The second everyone is out of sight we give a high five. The rest of the day is ours.

We head back the way we came, a quaint little pub our destination. After lunch, we will follow our footsteps to our house and put up the season's lights. If time allows, we will then drive into town for last-minute Christmas shopping before picking up the kids. The journey home is our own personal and private walk-about, during which we always touch something core in our relationship. We usually spent the time asking "How are we doing?" We also explore, "Is this the life we want, and are we still in love?" They are good walks.

It continues to snow, and already another four inches covers our old tracks. Holding hands and talking, it feels as if we are on our first date, without the nervousness. By the time we settle into the cozy warm surroundings of the pub, we conclude that we are indeed blessed. Sitting in our usual corner table by the fire and bay window, we order our yearly hot buttered rum. While watching the snow, I share my epiphany and explain that I seem to be involved in a journey of change. She asks, with a touch of concern in her voice, "Where is it taking you?"

"I don't know... yet." But I reassure her that our marriage is secure. When lunch finishes, we have answers to all the questions a couple should ask. Left unanswered are questions that only an individual can answer. Who am I, and what do I believe in?

After paying the bill, we leave—and I make sure to hold her hand where a squeeze of love comes through her fingers. We take a tributary path, and just before linking with our morning walk, we stop at a partially frozen pond. Someday, when our kids are old enough, I will bring them to our little hide-away for lunch and show them this place. We will tell them all about the times we stopped here, just so they know that part of our life. I look forward to that day.

Years ago, my soul-mate and I discovered that if we skip a stone on the ice it makes the most unusual sounds. Depending on the number of rocks tossed, and their weight, an amazing symphony occurs. Everybody, once in their life, should skip rocks on a partially frozen pond. It is truly remarkable.

In the silence, we sit throwing and listening, listening and throwing. I hug my wife and share, "We make beautiful music together." She laughs, and my heart soars. I feel young. I feel light. I look at her and she has a quizzical expression. "What?" I stammer.

"I haven't seen you look so happy in a long time. You've been so, I don't know, sad lately. It's like you're being crushed with worry or exhaustion."

I continue throwing rocks while trying to formulate an answer. I throw big stones and small pebbles looking for the right words. My wife continues, "Is it the epiphany you had on your run that's bothering you?"

I nod. "It's partially that, but it's also one of my students." While skipping stones and listening to what they have to say, I realize Penny is on my mind more than I want to acknowledge. "I wish I had seen her the last day of school. I just feel I'm not reaching her."

"What would you have said to her?"

My pathetic response is a shrug, "I honestly don't know."

I am chided when she adds, "That's unlike you. You're a better teacher than that. Besides, there's always a Penny, someone who won't accept help." She means her comment to be supportive, but it has the opposite effect. I know that this is not

Penny's fault. Have I even tried? Somewhere, deep in my sub-conscious, a feeling grows—a warning that I cannot quite hear, or a premonition that I do not want to accept, but deep down, I know what it means; change is coming.

My wife groans, "See, there it is again! That look... you look so tired sometimes." This time I feel the dread. Silently, we hold hands and walk away from the lake.

While we walk, I share that I have genuinely missed Penny during that last class. An odd feeling, I admit. Usually the students that attend are the students I teach. I have no time to reach out to those who cannot bother. The train just moves too damn fast. As we stroll, arm in arm, I share my trepidation and she helps bring everything to the surface. I know that she understands when I share, "None of this will adversely affect our marriage. Maybe when I work through it all, who knows, it might even help." She squeezes herself close. It is a sign of her trust.

I continue. "For the first time, I'm having a bit of a crisis at work. I'm confused and have lost my bottom line. I have no vision, and no one around me has one either. We have gone from the schoolhouse to the warehouse, and are heading to-wards the outhouse. It's all so polarized, so political. All we do is cover our ass. Education only works if the government supports the school district who supports the administrators, and they support teachers, and we in turn support students. Otherwise, we are just constantly reacting and never leading in the field where we are supposed to be the experts."

It helps to hear her say, "I think I'm starting to under-stand. Maybe Penny represents all the children you feel you're not reaching, the ones that the education system fails." I walk in silence, thinking.

We arrive home far too quickly, but my wife and I have a good old-fashioned stress-releasing snowball fight—ending the walk like a couple of kids, laughing and rolling in the snow. With our walk-about done, I feel a closer relationship.

Within me however, the specter of dread remains. Even this might in fact be good fortune, if I have the courage to deal with it.

We put up the Christmas lights, so that when the kids arrive our house is in all its seasonal glory. Then, we head into town for last minute stocking-stuffers. For one of the few times over the holidays, we leave our winter wonderland and are soon in the brown slush of the city. Our shopping is swift and accurate, and we head back as fast as possible to our blanketed paradise.

Swinging by our neighbors, we pick up our kids, who are too sleepy to regurgitate the day's events. That most assuredly will happen tomorrow. Letting us know he survived the day, Lab releases a loud groan from the back seat. Our children miss the view of our glittering lights as we carry them asleep into the house.

Once the kids are tucked in, my loving wife brings me a hot chocolate and announces, "I know you want to stay up, but I'm exhausted."

"Sleep well and thanks, not just for the drink but for everything."

Her response comes in the form of a wink, reminding me of the young girl that I first fell in love with. She whispers from the loft, "Don't think too long about Penny; it will all work out. You're a good teacher."

I sit in our study with one small light on, and Lab faithfully curled beside me, his head on my lap. My ever so intuitive wife knows that I will be thinking about Penny. This is the case, not just because of what we discussed, but also due to an incident while we shopped.

We were walking through the mall when we turned a corner and I came face-to-face with my student, Penny. She pretended not to recognize me. I had the beginnings of a hello but could not find the end of it. We approached each other so closely that not even a pebble could pass between us.

She continued on and I watched while she met some friends. I recognized some faces, and was disturbed since a couple of them were seriously involved in drugs. I was not sure what group she would choose for friends, but this reality was sad to see. I know that the kids she met used the needle, and now, for the first time, I wonder if Penny does as well.

My relationship with her is so superficial that I have no idea how to approach this. It is devastating to realize that if I can't even wish her Merry Christmas, how can I ever help her if she's doing drugs? In my short career, I have seen many students drop out because of that world. I have to admit however, that it has never bothered me to this degree. With so many faces to teach, the ugly truth is, having one less student often helps. For some reason, this one student matters.

How can I help her? I am her teacher, but our association is nonexistent; she does not even acknowledge me, and I have to accept that I do not acknowledge her.

I had a wonderful day today, yet feel insignificant and undefined. Appropriately, Lab groans and gets off the couch, leaving me for his bed. I am alone. I think of building a fire, not for the warmth, but for its reflections on the walls. With my shadow dancing about, my sense of desolation will somehow be less real. I look around and feel lost, as if dread sits with me, and will forever, if I do not act. It is here and now that I realize this must all change! I do not want to live in fear!

This will only happen when I know who I am and what I believe in. If I cannot accomplish this, Penny may never see me—and I will assuredly never know her.

Chapter 15

The wisdom of enlightenment is inherent in every one of us. It is because of the delusion under which our mind works that we fail to realize it ourselves, and that we have to seek the advice and the guidance of enlightened ones.
~Hui-Neng

As predicted, our kids awaken and promptly share yesterday's adventure. Of course, all this takes place before my wife and I are even out of bed. The big event is that our neighbor's deem them old enough to take the reins of the sleigh. I like that my kids have taken control of a horse before driving our estate car. That's the car that all country children drive first, the old beater that never leaves the "estate."

They also heard a wolf. Apparently, because of some deep ancestral memory, Lab answered back with a howl. I wish I had been there for both those events.

Today is born crystal clear and icicle cold. Despite this, we take our children to the local Christmas craft fair. The bitter cold gives my jeep plenty to complain about all the way down the driveway. Despite the engine's grumbled mutterings and the deep snow, we make it to the local community hall. For the craft fair, people's transportation varies from four-wheel drives to cross country skis. In this harbor, every major social event occurs here. More a barn than a proper building, this structure has seen it all. One night it is used as a combination jazz-jam, potluck dinner locale, the next night it's a wedding hall. Most locals have had their first kiss here as well as their first fight—often on the same night.

Once inside, I let go of my children's hands and allow them to run free, knowing that they are safe among friends and neighbors. While they race off to see classmates and dodge in and out of customers, I watch my wife from across the hall. While I remember all the events that we have enjoyed here, she looks up and catches me watching her. With an odd expression, she waves. She also winks at me, and at that moment I do not think I have ever loved anybody more in my life. Why then, why that moment? I am not sure. It may have to do with yesterday's walk-about. My walls are small, and she seems to sense this as we walk towards each other.

Just then, I do something that I have never done before. I put my arms around her and kiss her both publicly and passionately. With her pressed close, I feel she understands. I am declaring my love for her, for all our friends, acquaintances and neighbors to see.

In time, we again feel the people around us. She gives me the biggest smile imaginable and says, "That look you have on your face right now, it suits you." I do not know how I appear, but I do feel as if I am seventeen again and in love—that first love, where you have not developed any walls yet, and are completely vulnerable. The type of love that, when it is over, you know you will have a broken heart and in time you will learn that it is no one's fault.

For the rest of the day we hold hands, and in time gather

our children and celebrate. They have found their Holy Grail—a special present for someone on Christmas day.

Once we arrive home the weather turns even colder, but at least our stomachs are full of all the cookies and fudge we bought for that night's dessert. We remind our kids that we have already eaten dessert, and do not want to hear any complaints after dinner. My youngest son is fine with this, and I fully believe he will live his life with an "Eat dessert first because you could choke and not get to the good stuff" philosophy.

Once we dash in from the cold, my wife turns and gives me a huge hug. The kids shout, "Group hug," and join in. Whenever this family moment occurs, Lab's nails are heard slipping on the floor as he scampers to stand on his hind legs and join in. We make quite the sight, five humans and a wannabe in a circle hugging, one lone tail wagging.

After dinner, I decide that this is my night to go and cut down the chosen Christmas tree. Some years I wait for a snowstorm, or like this year a cold, crisp, clear evening tells me that it is time to venture out alone. I would prefer a full moon to light my way, but this year only a crescent slice will be my companion. I take my kid's 'Snow Rocket' to tie the tree to, and say my good-byes. Before setting off, my wife slips our cell-phone into my pocket, spoiling some of my adventure.

Lab volunteers to sprawl by the fire and make sure my family is safe. I chuckle at his loyalty.

Once outside, my breath is taken away—partially by the bone-chilling cold, but mainly by the night sky. Stars dominate the pitch black, thus making me feel even smaller. Alone in a crowded universe. I cherish that feeling. Small in a galaxy of one hundred billion stars, let alone the billions of other galaxies. This does not even count the literally countless planets, moons, asteroids and just stuff that may or may not include aliens and all their possessions. Walking along the country road, I feel the night silence and stars plead with my soul for acknowledgement.

It is such a clear night that even without moonlight the trail is easy to follow. It is the coldest day of the year, and the snow is at least two feet deep with the surface frozen so that it crunches under foot. The cold attacks my nostrils, but my instincts tell me I have chosen the right night. I consider returning for my snowshoes, but with the discipline running has given me I find a comfortable stride, and in time, my body warms to the task.

Like a hard run, walking in these conditions can be a very meditative experience. The more lost in thought one becomes, the easier the effort. There is so much for me to think about in my solitude that both time and distance pass quickly. It feels as if I am earning the privilege of clarity within my life.

I recall camping with "at risk" students. A frigid night like this, and their fire the only thing keeping us warm. I took some brave souls for a hike to warm up, while those too wimpy or just too "cool" to move remained behind. I had warned them to keep that fire going as the temperature was dropping and soon it might be impossible to light again. When we return, properly warmed from our hike, I was stunned to see shivering youths standing around nudging the last of the faint embers with their boots. Just as I was about to yell at their laziness it dawned on me that I was actually seeing just what few life-skills these kids actually had. They literally were too lazy, or dysfunctional, or unaware, to even keep a life-giving fire going. I had to work fast to get the already cut firewood into the last of the heat. Another few minutes and we would have spent the night without warmth. After it got going, I did not even bother to lecture about the need for a fire.

I contemplate Penny and wonder what skills she has, if any.

I see my life's journey, and with each step feel an understanding of why I have arrived at this point. Many of my career and personal decisions come from a perspective of fear. All too often, I make the decision that is safest or most secure. I never make decisions based on passion or dreams, and sadly this assures that my dreams and passions will be unfulfilled. Instead of disappointment at this revelation, I am oddly encouraged and enlightened. The first step often is acknowledgement; one never begins a journey until there is an understanding that a journey is needed.

Deeper into the forest, it has become so dark that I can easily imagine the trees themselves drinking the light from the night sky. The only remaining light is directly above as the forest closes on either side. The stars above take on the form of a river of lights that bend and curve with the trail. It is actually easier to follow the path by looking up and allowing the light-river to guide. This gives the sensation that my life, is for the moment, turned upside down.

This experience motivates me to think of the most grounded person I know, the Scottish teacher who talked with Penny about words having weight. When a gust of wind from the mountains cuts through me, it is warming to think of him. I recall the time he asked, "Why are you a teacher and what gives you the right?" Thinking of this somehow gives me strength, and I almost laugh at the wind for trying to make me cold. I do not feel weak, tired, or heavy: I feel alive.

For a moment in my walk, I never even notice the cold. For a short distance, I am beyond the weather. I replay a story that he once shared in the staff room, about when he was in the Navy. While serving on an aircraft carrier, he was working on a ladder when he slipped and fell, not just off the ladder but also off the aircraft carrier! After fishing him and the ladder out of the water he was told, "The Captain wants to see you. Immediately!" A summoning by the Captain of a ship this size is a big deal and he did not even stop to see the ship's doctor or get dry clothes.

Standing in soaking wet clothes, dripping on the captain's deck, he is asked, "Are you alright?"

Apparently, he would have answered "Fine, Captain," even if he'd had a broken leg.

"Well," the Captain growls, "It has just been reported that you're trying to steal ladders off my ship!" Despite his amazingly agile mind for one of the few times in his life my Scottish colleague was speechless. Then the Captain broke out laughing and slaps him on the back, saying: "Glad you're safe. Go get dried off."

Despite the cold and being alone, I too break out laughing. I stand there, all alone laughing, when I should have been bent over and shivering. I am shockingly comfortable.

It is then that I remember that I am still on a mission. Following my markers, I find the chosen tree. As I squat in the snow, my saw cuts and I earn the right to yell "Timber!" as all four feet of my tree topples. Feeling satisfied, I take a drink from my water bottle. I luxuriate in my world, when suddenly a haunting light flows through and around the tops of trees. It looks as if the forest has a halo!

I set my water bottle down and wander toward the ghostly glow. It flickers, dances and changes color. I have never seen anything like it, eerie and magnificent at the same time. It is there and then it is gone and then back again. On all fours, I crawl over a small rise and the forest gives way to a small pasture. The stars are so close that it looks as if I can rake my fingers through them, creating trails of star clusters and swirls of circular galaxies, bump stars out of orbit or grab spiral galaxies by the tail and whip them towards another constellation. In the east, the supernatural light dominates the horizon. Then it is gone. In an instant it is back, this time over the entire sky. Then, in a moment, it is not. Stars appear sparkling and bright—and then disappear as from horizon to horizon, the sky turns green.

I sit in silence and watch with amazement. The Northern Lights usually do not show themselves this far south. So in solitude and awe I watch the celestial show. It is the first time I have ever seen them. Sitting at peace, I grasp the full impact of my first epiphany. My ego must first build walls of denial so that it can survive. But these walls must be torn down so that I may live. For this to happen, I must realize that there are things bigger than myself. For me to understand, I have to stand under these stars and this vision.

With incalculable stars and colors beyond my ability to imagine, it reinforces for me how tiny I actually am. As I sit here, it is all so simple; it is not difficult at all. I really am small. Frustrated that I can only stay a moment, which has already been three, I need to start my journey home since there is a family who will soon begin worrying.

I tie the little tree to the sled then wrap the rope around my waist. However, before departing, I look again and acknowledge what I know. All alone, it is unmistakable. I am getting closer to answering, "Who am I and what do I believe in?" Just feeling closer to this answer gives me energy.

I start back the nearly two kilometers. During this entire trip, at no time am I cold or even tired. Soon I see the lights of my home, and in many ways they are as beautiful as the aureole borealis. In a few minutes, we will be decorating our chosen tree.

The next morning is Christmas Day, and it is all that I can dream: a white Christmas, children just the right age, and my wife happy. I experience inner peace now more than any other time in my life. It has been a perfect day, and yet the night somehow exceeds the day. After dinner I ask my kids if they want an adventure, and they squeal with delight. If my kids will take a chance on the unknown, rather than sitting playing with their new toys—or worse, watching television—as their father, I am doing something right.

It is too cold to go far, so we bundle up and climb a small hill in our back yard. With the house lights off, I hear my Dad's voice as I tell my kids, "Look up." The previous night's display is still shimmering. My two sons and daughter sit silent, in heavenly awe. My wife and I sit content, watching our children—their mouths and, I hope, their minds and hearts open, feeling small and significant. We sit as a family. Even Lab sits respectfully, the Northern Lights reflecting in the bowl clenched tightly in his mouth.

Chapter 16

This, then, is the human problem; there is a price to be paid for every increase in consciousness. We cannot be more sensitive to pleasure without being more sensitive to pain.
~Alan Watts

The holidays continued, as did the great fun. The falling snow returned, and after days of trying to keep up, we succumbed.

Our driveway piled high with white, dictating that we are going nowhere. I find it amazing how quickly our priorities change when circumstances influence events. All of a sudden, all we care about is that the wood supply is dry and that the back-up generator is full. We check on the old couple down the lane and promise that we will return.

Being snowbound is enriching, and our log home adds to this. Whenever the seasons test us, the logs not only act as a physical barrier but a psychological buffer as well. When we eventually lose power, I choose not to turn the generator on in case the outage lasts for an extended period. For simple two-day blackouts we are battle-hardened and prepared. I will never understand how families share these experiences in the city's mega-homes. In one of those places, family members could hide from one another for a month. Our fireplace acts as the natural spot for the family to gravitate toward, and it provides everything we need.

On one of these non-electrical days I walk Lab, aiming for our old neighbors, when some friends pass on cross-country skis. They warn about a ferocious weather system coming, an ice storm, the first to hit the area in sixty years. I am glad that I picked today to again check in on our old friends.

They are fine, and I am proud of our little community. Someone else has already cleared their driveway. We sit chatting, and while warming myself near their fire, I gaze out the window to see a generous pile of freshly chopped wood. Someone has indeed been working hard to make sure that they are well looked after. They are good people, and when I leave I have a container of cake for my children and a warm feeling inside.

While walking home, I hear the familiar clanging of Swiss sleigh-bells. My other neighbors offer a free ride. Lab has not even waited for the invitation, as I look up embarrassed to see him already sitting in the sleigh's seat. I shrug and climb in chuckling, "Do I have a choice?"

We talk about the coming weather and they ask, "Ever been in an ice storm?"

"No," I answer, "but my Dad has. They sound very exotic."

"Exotic!" they guffaw. "Maybe terrifying, scary for sure, but can't say we'd use the word exotic."

After they drop us off, they snap the reins and head home—but not before advising, "Power won't be coming back on tonight. It will be a few days at least—make sure you have lots of firewood." I am beginning to grasp why so many people are looking after our old neighbors.

That night the temperature plummets, forcing us to bring out our heavy 'Hudson Bay' blankets.

While doing chores the next morning, I note there is something unusual about the day's weather. I cannot put my finger on it, but the grays are grayer and the clouds not quite in their expected places. Even the color of the water in the harbor is not entirely correct. It shimmers silver, looking more like a pool of mercury than a protected harbor. By noon nothing has changed, and for this coastal location that is a rarity. Living here means expecting weather changes every fifteen minutes. I have seen it snow on my house with nothing but blue sky above. The only explanation is that it must have blown off the mountains. Even double rainbows, that either begin or end on an island in the middle of the bay, are common. Our windstorms are the stuff of legend, but today's weather strikes a chord between calm and threatening. It is all very ominous.

This area of the country has the nickname "Venice of the North" due to all the busy water traffic. Today however, the fishing and charter boats are only entering the bay, none exit, as they search for protection. The little skiffs and runabouts that everyone here uses for shopping and errands, are securely tied. Even the local water-taxi that ferries late night drinkers from the pub is not running. Without the taxi, and with most roads closed due to ice and snow, the pub will be quiet tonight.

When I finish securing our house, I share with my wife what I think is a brilliant idea. She quickly and not so eloquently downsizes my proposal to "stupid." My now somewhat less than "brilliant" idea is to experience the ice storm, "first hand." After dinner I will walk down to the pub, which I am sure will be empty, and have a hot rum, then head home. She again uses the dreaded, "S" word. Even a promise that I will be cautious, and if it becomes dangerous I'll turn back, does not stop her from muttering something about "men." I choose not to ask her to repeat it.

With the use of our back-up generator, we eat an early dinner. Outside, there is already a solid wall of sleet falling sideways. From our window, you can see ice building up on the woodshed and clothesline. I make sure there is a good fire and that my family has lots of firewood inside before I set out. I have absolute faith that my log home will protect them.

I give myself a timeline of five hours to get there, have a hot drink and return. My wife knows that will be plenty of time. Lab bravely volunteers to protect the family from his spot in front of the fireplace, on his back, staring at the ceiling, with all four paws stretching into the air. It is his alert position in case of intruders, or so I choose to believe.

I kiss my wife good-bye, even though she presents a moving target as her head shakes back and forth all the while muttering "Testosterone poisoning." With my snowshoes and best Gore-Tex for protection, and a non-negotiable cell phone in my pocket, I set out for the solitude of the pub.

The second I am outside my jacket is starched stiff by ice. My "brilliant" idea, gets immediately downgraded, but I still think that it is a long way from, "stupid."

I instantly realize that I have never been exposed to this type of weather. However, pride alone dictates that I at least get to the end of the driveway before turning back. Halfway down, I look back at my familiar landscape—but I do not recognize any of it. It is as if a scene from Dr. Zhivago is in my backyard. It is actually quite stunning, if not for the stinging pellets of ice slashing across my face. Everywhere I look, it is one large icicle. My home appears more like an igloo than a log structure. One can easily imagine the next ice age. A month of this, and civilization as we know it would easily be wiped out.

Even I acknowledge that this is definitely not an idea that falls into the "brilliant" category. Only the soft yellow candlelight streaming from the window gives any indication of warmth. Even the smoke coming from the chimney appears to freeze motionless over the house.

Stubborn pride alone forces me to the end of the driveway. My wool pants covered with Gore-Tex are having difficulty bending at the knees. I walk like one of the robots from a 1950's sci-fi movie. All I have to do, if I can, is raise my arms straight out and I will be an Arctic version of The Mummy. At the bottom of the driveway, I can no longer see my house and am even having difficulty opening my eyes as ice begins to cover my face. This is now officially a, "stupid" idea. How do women have such insight? If I could, I would shrug as I lean into the biting wind and move forward.

The frozen world that encases my house is not so slowly assimilating me. What really motivates me to do this "stupid" thing is that I need to be by myself. At least that is what my slowly freezing brain tells my already frozen legs. My legs and brain have a rather belligerent conversation regarding male pride and losing face with my family. Speaking of losing face... I take my gloved hand and wipe off a mask of ice. The unfrozen part of my brain wins and my legs struggle towards the pub.

My running discipline convinces me that I can do this. I think to myself maybe I should give up running. A couch potato would never find himself in this situation. I try to smile, but my frozen face fails as I recall the sailor's proverb: "He that would go to sea for pleasure, would go to hell for a pastime." It occurs to me that I am not a sailor but somehow it does seem appropriate that I am going for a drink of rum, even if it is the hot buttered kind. Forward I go, but I am aware enough to go only as far as is safe, which coincidently I correlate as the same distance as my destination. Doesn't hypothermia affect the cognitive processes?

The sound of snow crunching under foot as my snowshoes grip is all I hear other than the constant wind. Between crunches is a desperate howl. Crunch... howl... crunch.... howl. Nothing else matters.

It is dark and the treetops vanish into low clouds. Frozen rain slices at my face when I look up. I am very quickly deep into my first ice storm. The peak of my baseball cap juts out from under my hood and offers protection as long as I keep my head down. This gives me the distinct feeling of bowing to the power of the storm. My little harbor can now easily be mistaken for the high mountains of Tibet.

Occasionally, a tree limb cracks off under the mass of ice. Other loud thumps are heard when ice, tugged by its weight, falls to the ground. It is brutally hard, but my desire to push myself propels my legs forward. I am lucky that I know my way, as all markers and familiar landmarks are simply gone. It is very disorientating, and I am tempted by an old Indian saying: "If you walk backwards you can never be lost."

Fortunately this is a trail I have walked often, and I eventually arrive exhausted at my destination. The effort has been extreme. Drained, I finally lift my heavy legs up the steps to the pub's entrance. I do not know which beckons more: hot rum, a seat, or the warm fire. I remove my snowshoes and stomp off as much ice as possible. It falls from my shoulders in one sheet, shattering on the concrete steps. Inside, as expected, I am alone in a room lit only by a crackling fire.

With no lights, the fire throws the shadows from the chairs and tables dancing upon the walls and ceiling. It looks as if whoever last sat in this room all left at once, abandoning their shadows to do a mad, frantic, angst-dance. It is unsettling, since many of the shadows look like Edvard Munch's "The

Scream." I have the strangest feeling that they are all waiting for me, madly dancing because I have finally arrived. It is most unnerving.

I sit close to the fire, and shadows shimmer up the wall and stretch across the ceiling. While the shadows mock me, outside the wind howls. My unease does not abate when a waitress appears from behind an unseen door, and looks startled to see someone sitting in her pub. She looks at me as if I was crazy, and I stare back, making sure that she is not a shadow manifesting into human form. I try a smile to alleviate her concern, but my facial muscles stopped working an hour ago. I worry that I look like an actor with a face full of Botox, trying to appear younger, but instead just looking alien.

Thankfully she speaks first. "Goodness, you must be thirsty to come out on a night like this! I live in the back rooms, and even I don't want to be here tonight." Sitting near the fire I realize how absurd I must look, and decide that it would be best not to try and explain. Besides, after just one drink when I put my snowshoes and jacket back on and walk back out into those conditions, I'll look even more absurd. Maybe I should have listened to my wife.

When the waitress takes my order she also fulfills the Woman's Union Agreement by mumbling, "Coming here for a drink on a night like this isn't the brightest thing you have ever done."

I smile and say the word that she wants to use, but knows that if she does there will be no tip. "Yes, it was probably stupid of me."

This seems to fulfill her contractual agreement with the Woman's Union, and she repeats my order. "Hot buttered rum… got it." She examines my melting form and, sadly, cannot resist. "Would you like ice with that?"

I smile, and mutter politely, "No, thank you."

She disappears behind the counter, and I hear a male voice explode with laughter: "Tonight... in this... stupid idiot!"

My brain wants to shout "Traitor!"—but it is already lost in the flickering flames of the roaring fire. It is difficult to relax with the insanely dancing shadows and the odd scraping noise emanating from the metal roof. Occasionally, ice slides down ending in a heavy thump as it shatters on the ground.

My drink arrives, and she winks. "Made it a double, no extra cost. Have to respect a man who can handle this weather."

Too late... I think to myself, but instead I say, "Thank you kindly."

As she leaves me to be accosted by the shadow dancers, I notice my drink begins shaking in my hand. Next, I feel a pain in my fingers as if thousands of needles are stabbing. It is excruciating. My hands involuntarily tremble as they feel the warmth from the fire. Then the shadows begin mocking me in earnest. They whirl frantically, and my sips turn into two large gulps. I stare at the fire. I experience what there is to experience, and am grateful for what is there: the storm, the fire, the angst-dancing shadows. I leave a large tip.

It seems to take forever to hoist on my heavy jacket, as if the shadows themselves grab it, preventing me from leaving. Eventually, I flee while the shadows slide and stretch over the chairs and floor. The most hysterical ones scrape at the walls and ceilings. Struggling with my gloves, my hands shake violently. I realize I have been sitting too close to the fire, and my hands are still accustomed to the cold. When I open the door to flee, shadows contort even more fanatically as cold air rushes in to feed the flames. I close the door, but not before looking back at the frenzied shadow-dance. I have to look away.

It is so cold outside that my clothes instantly become rigid, and I set a pace to get home as quickly as possible. The sleet has stopped, and it takes me a moment to realize there is no precipitation or sound of any kind. The howling wind has ceased. It is frigid cold and absolutely calm. My hand stings, but the cold numbs the thousand needles. Walking home will be difficult enough without having to shake and flex my fingers through frozen gloves.

While walking in the quiet, I hear a faint sound unlike anything that I have heard before. I stop to listen, and the sound stops. A few steps, and I hear it again. It's faint and extremely delicate, impossible to tell if it is near or far away. I stop again, and again so does it. I start, and it starts. It sounds like a miniature glass wind-chime moving ever so lightly, or perhaps hummingbird wings shattering. Somehow, my movement creates this sound. It is a very subtle tinkling. If angel wings were ever heard, this is how they would sound.

While I listen, I remember my Dad telling me he experienced this phenomenon during his ice storm. The moisture in the air is frozen, and I am literally cracking it when I walk. It is as beautiful a sound as I have ever been fortunate enough to hear. I am breaking the air by walking through it.

However, stopping to appreciate the tinkling causes the pain in my hand to will itself to the forefront of my consciousness. This pain feels so much like needles that I am forced to reflect on Penny. The thought of her using the needle hurts even more than my hand. I do not know if it is the intensity of my ice storm escapade, or acknowledging my deep sadness for Penny, but I only realize now that something is missing from my trail. The paddle-shaped footprints from my snowshoes are gone. The trail has completely vanished under a duvet of white. With no imprint to show that I have been this way, I half laugh wondering if I turn around once more, will I be gone?

I was going to use the footprints to help navigate my way home. I know these trails like the back of my hand, but this storm has now covered all familiar markers. All the trees look the same, like white ice cream cones. Sections of the trail are discernable, but I worry if I can find my way.

It takes deep concentration to keep my mind off the pain in my hand and stay within the safety of the trail. Each step cracks the hard frozen surface until the softer snow cushions my snowshoes, enabling me to stride. Trying to keep focus, I closely observe each step. This concentration wills my attention on each stride rather than my predicament. In turn, I become more aware and notice little worlds that I would normally miss. I observe miniscule jewels of frozen snow fly into the air from the initial impact of each step. They fly until gravity calls, and then like mini-meteors they plunge back to the surface of earth. Upon impact each meteor shatters into thousands of even smaller ice-pearls. My second epiphany has begun.

These ice-pearls are unlike the shoulder-shaking rocks of my mountain epiphany. There I was releasing something, making room for something else. I quickly realize that the ice-pearls represent reality. I cannot deny the reality that I am in pain. I cannot deny the reality of the ice storm. Most importantly, I can no longer deny my deep concern for Penny.

In the cold and wild of the night, it is as if a veil is ripped away. The shadows will remain behind in the pub, doing their dance forever. I will now face the rest of my journey alone. My shadow is now gone—most likely never to return. Feel the pain!

In my mind's eye, I see Penny with a needle stuck in her arm and my hand screams as if she stuck a dull, used, needle into me. I watch as she sharpens the blunted point of the needle on a pack of matches, scraping it along the part that you strike, scraping until it regains some of its sharpness—then jabbing its semi-dull point into her vein until its contents flow. My ice-pearls continue shattering on the ground while my hand vibrates in agony. I can feel Penny's pain.

With each step comes a deeper understanding of a simple reality. No matter how much I want my shadow to help me stay immune, it simply is no longer possible. I care about Penny. I exist.

My first epiphany has made my ego smaller, making room for consciousness, and thus earning me the privilege of a second epiphany that forces me to acknowledge reality. At a very basic level, I accept that this life is not a dress rehearsal for what may come. This is the real thing! I can no longer hide behind my wall of immunity that denial gives me. I must step forward and participate in life. Choice has helped me move from shadow to substance, but now that I am substance I no longer have a choice.

The air continues to shatter as I walk through it. Suppressing my ego by abandoning the rocks, or the words that society has given me, and standing under something larger than myself—the stars and Northern Lights—help make room for this simple wisdom... I exist! I no longer choose just to survive life. I choose to live it. I choose reality! My walls of denial are breaking apart like the fragile frozen ice-pearls that shatter on the surface of the planet. In this ice storm, I choose life over survival. With each thought the pain in my hand intensifies.

When the storm obliterated my footprints, it was as if I was never here. Walking home completely alone, without my shadow, without even an imprint of having passed this way, my epiphany ends when I realize that I exist now for the very first time. I know this to be true because of what has become important to me. I can now answer the question "Who are you and what do you believe in?"

Turning into my driveway, I am a solid mass of ice; my feet sting, my face is frozen and my hand hurts beyond words. My knees are unable to bend and my jacket arms cannot flex.

I look like the abominable snowman. I should be heavy with fatigue, but instead I feel light and energetic.

As I enter my home, my wife greets me. "How was..." She stops and stares, hardly recognizing the white mound that stands grinning like an idiot before her. She looks deeply into my eyes.

I answer the question she cannot formulate. "I know who I am." Her head tilts as she realizes my face still has tears frozen on it. "I am a man who cares!"

She smiles, confused, and mutters, "Honey, I have always known that is who you are."

I laugh almost hysterically. "But don't you see? You love me. I have never been able to love myself. So how could I have known who I am? But now I do. I am a man who cares, and I believe in myself." She watches as frozen tears begin to melt and run down my face. I begin thawing, and my heart warms. "You don't understand do you?" She shakes her head, so I explain. "I can help Penny now." Her eyes reveal confusion. "I can... I could always... I have something to offer her now. I couldn't reach her, or any of those other kids, until I loved myself. Sweetheart, don't you see? I have earned the right."

Then it hit me, the rest of my second epiphany. I hear the Scottish teacher's voice asking, "Why are you a teacher, and what gives you the right?"

I grab my wife and hug her. She startles from the cold and wet of my clothes, but I feel her return my hug. "I have paid the price to know who I am and what I believe in... I care... that is why I am a teacher, and why I have earned the right!"

Chapter 17

There is no royal road to anything. One thing at a time, and all things in succession. That which grows slowly, endures.
~Joshua Holland

On my last day of holidays, because of all the sleighs and cross-country skiers leaving grooves in the road, I am able to go for a run. Jogging carefully along the slippery empty road, I am involved in an event that ends the holidays with a smile. Running past the now completely frozen lakes, I see many of the local kids enjoying a last game of hockey. The younger children either watch enviously from the perimeter or skate in a separate area with the assistance of parents. The smoke from the community's fireplaces drifts lazily along the ice and mingles with the players. Some of the faster skaters drag and swirl the smoke, creating mystical images. My winter running clothes keep me physically warm while the scene I observe warms my heart.

Some tots, with ice skates tied around their necks and holding hands with parents, are struggling across the road. Out of the corner of my eye, I notice a family of deer preparing to dart out of the woods. I stop running and hold my arm in the air so the pedestrians will stop and not startle the deer. The family of deer crosses on cue, literally under my arm. When I begin running again I look at the people waiting to cross.

That is when I notice him. A little boy, younger than the others, is watching me with an open mouth. All the other heads swivel in the direction of the deer as they lope away. I glance back and, just before rounding a corner, I can still see the little boy's open mouth gawk while dad tugs at his arm encouraging him to cross the road. The boy's right arm is raised as he points as if he knows me. It is obvious even from a distance he has no intention of moving until I am out of sight.

I wonder why I deserve the look of uninhibited awe from that youngster. Then, in mid-stride, it occurs to me. I am wearing a red jacket and red running pants, am sprouting a scruffy holiday beard, and have just helped "Rudolph" cross the road. That little boy has just seen Santa in the flesh. "Santa" is out for a run, trying to get in shape after the Christmas season. It is the only explanation for ten heads watching the deer and one little boy looking in the opposite direction. It's the perfect ending to a wonderful holiday.

School starts tomorrow, so this night my bed will greet me early. Just before falling asleep, I give sincere thanks for all that I have experienced and for all that I have. It is then that the realization comes that I feel so fundamentally changed—I have not even acknowledged my lack of dread.

Starting my jeep's engine the next morning, I feel as if the whole world has changed. I maneuver down the driveway, fully aware that I have energy and a sense of purpose. During my drive to work, I wonder if the triviality of "everydayness" motivates the ego's walls, making shadow strong. None of my holiday was trivial, as every moment had purpose. I did not need to use energy to defend ego, and therefore be tired all the time.

Driving to work after the time spent with my family, the fun of snowball fights, hikes, ice storms, and of course epiphanies, I feel I have transcended everyday trivia. This allows me to evolve beyond most of my ego. I have entered the time of the in-between. In the rarified realm of choice, this is the time that lies between substance and that which is to come.

My first test comes immediately upon entering the city—and in an all-too-familiar way, a driver cuts me off and gives me the finger. My first instinct fills me not with rage but with awe and empowerment. I have no reaction! I look right into eyes of the enraged person who is jabbing "that" finger into the air. In his eyes, despite an almost out-of-body anger, he reminds me of an empty vessel. It is as if I am in a canoe, when suddenly another canoe floating on the same current bumps into me—except the other vessel is empty. Would I yell at or let an empty canoe upset me? No, I would move on as if nothing happened. In all reality, there cannot be an exchange between us because "us" does not exist. Realizing all this, I simply drive on while the empty vessel beside me insanely rages. Inside, I feel no anger or frustration, nor even fatigue.

I arrive at the school's early morning staff meeting, and as soon as it begins, I am shocked at what I observe. The moment the administrator starts talking, nearly every teacher turns and begins a side conversation or shuffling through paper. Only one does not, the person that I had decided to ask to be my mentor: the Scottish teacher. He sits looking directly at me with the oddest expression. I interpret his look as one of part pride, part curiosity.

The meeting continues, and I wonder if all the meetings have been like this. Had I been like this? No one listens. It is as if they are saying, "Just get us the textbooks, and let us out of this room so we can do our shift. The God Curriculum is our savior and our reason for being." The administrator uses terms like "Great year," and "Best school." These terms are so hollow they have no meaning. I quizzically look back at my possible mentor as he continues studying me.

Leaving the meeting, I feel awkward and out of place. I cannot get his expression out of my mind. On my way to class, I try to say, "Hello," to as many students as I can. Some respond while others do not comprehend. When passing my colleagues I ask, "How were your holidays?" Interestingly, some respond while others do not comprehend. I decide that the next day I will try again. I choose not to be ignored. I will not just go away. I cannot go away because I now exist. I have made the evolutionary leap from "Shadow" to "Substance."

It is only now that I begin to fully understand the degree to which I had retreated into my classroom. I am also realizing the level to which I had retreated into the safety of my "shadow." It is as if a firewall separated me from reality, and therefore my colleagues, and more importantly from my students. It is going to be a tough wall to break through.

I may have been giving the Scottish teacher too much credit, but his expression makes me believe he intuitively knows I have broken through the walls protecting my ego. I am now in the process of learning how to deal with reality; the walls that separated me from myself are being ripped away. All day I have energy, and work hard to help my students feel acknowledged when attending my class.

I feel deep sadness that Penny failed to attend. I am sincerely looking forward to seeing her. Shockingly, this sadness actually makes me feel good. In the past, my fatigue would have returned and the day would end in fear. Today this sadness makes me realize that this is just part of caring. It is simply the price one pays to participate in life.

The school day ends on an amazing and whimsical note. The staff parking lot is sloped, and is now a frozen sheet of ice. It is surrealistic to come out at the end of the day and find that all the cars are gone. It takes a moment to realize they have gathered at the lowest point in the parking lot. Despite emergency brakes and snow tires, they must have all just slowly slid to the bottom. They are all scattered in different directions, and magically have not hit each other. The Scottish teacher and I are standing beside each other, and he jokes, "They look like kid's toy cars left out in the backyard, just randomly tossed about." It is hard to accept what we are looking at. It is even harder to get all the cars turned and aimed at the exit.

While we are waiting, as we take turns spinning wheels and sliding toward home, my Scottish colleague rolls down his window. "I'm glad to see you had a great holiday."

"How do you know about my holiday?" I ask.

He just smiles ignoring my question and asks, "Have you seen Penny?"

"No," I answer, wondering why he asks specifically about her.

He then laughs. "Too bad. She's a great kid." Why is he reminding me of this? He looks directly into my eyes, laughs again, rolls up his window and drives off.

I then do a most peculiar thing. I turn my car back into the ice rink called a parking lot, and return to my class. I look up Penny's telephone number. I call, and am ready with caring words of concern and support. There is no answer. I leave a personal message on the impersonal machine, but am worried that my concern will not translate. I mention that I notice that she was not in school today and instead of chastising, I say that I missed her and hope that she is okay.

Driving home this night, I realize my day had been like all

other days—except, I am changed. The world has not changed; I have! I feel good, as if I am living a life full of purpose.

I have gone from my shadow into a world of choice. I should be tired, fatigued, since I am working harder, but miraculously the opposite is happening. I am feeling empowered, and this gives me access to a supply of energy I have never known. My first epiphany, when my ego became smaller, allowed for my second epiphany. Then I learned that I really am small, and my shadow is gone—hopefully forever. Now I can see and interact with reality. I have stepped out from behind the walls of ego into the world of reality, with choice lighting my way. I am now made of substance.

None of this has changed the world. It has only helped me know myself better.

The next day I rush to class, and the first thing I do is look for Penny. Sitting in her desk is her potential, still patiently waiting. There is no Penny to be seen.

Chapter 18

I saw Grief drinking a cup of sorrow and called out, "It tastes sweet, does it not?"

"You've caught me," Grief answered, "and you've ruined my business, how can I sell sorrow when you know it's a blessing?"

~Jalaluddin Rumi

Only days after my holidays ended, and the education train has already attained cruising speed. Cruising speed is just a notch above frantic, but just below hysterical, a speed where the conductors can no longer feel any bumps in the trip. Sitting in yet another meeting without a shadow to maintain my fog of unconsciousness, I realize how much time is given to discussing year-end activities. I question if we spend any time in the now. We practically never deal in the moment. Therefore, no matter how much planning and the best of intentions; seldom does the present receive any energy or attention. I sit questioning if we ever deal with reality. At times it looks as if the train conductor's hands are tied by the rigorous "Whenever I can get to it" schedule.

I have the disturbing thought that the train has only one focus and that is to reach the end. Which passengers get to their destination is irrelevant. The train MUST reach its last station, the end of the school year! After the meeting, I walk to class jostled by unconscious canoes as they drift past. There is a familiar message that comes over the public address system. Students from previous generations have all ignored the message, "No snowball fights on school property." I chuckle to myself as there is something gratifying about one generation ignoring another. Maybe, it gives us hope that we will not always make the same mistakes. Not only is my day good, but also my week is full of energy and teachable moments. I have made the conscious choice; the train may not care about the now, but I do.

Historically, I sleep in on the first weekend after the start of school. This Saturday however, I am radical and break with tradition. I rise early and enjoy the sunrise that is creeping over the mountains. Winter has lost most of its influence and the snowline is receding into the foothills. In another month, I will have reclaimed my mountain running trails. I look forward to those days.

It feels rewarding to have the energy to analyze how my year is going. When my ego was large, the best I could do was peak from behind its walls. I could only react, and did not have the capacity to deal with the now. It makes me wonder if this is why the collective that drives the train deals with the moment so poorly, if at all. Before, when I was in this state, paralyzed with fear, I could feel the composition of my life fall like dominoes. When the train experienced this, people scurried to their perspective rooms slamming the doors behind them. The noise of those doors closing was the sound of survival.

When my dominoes fell, it always began with frustration at work, then anger on the way home; waiting at home was the sense that my life was going in a direction that was not my choice, and accompanied by fatigue. When the dominoes fell for the train however, it reacted differently to the same crises. It just sped up, all the while declaring more success. I realize now why every day I returned home exhausted, feeling as if a train had run over me.

I can now investigate the rage I used to feel, that held me down for days and weeks at a time. It is clear that it all came about because my life was not moving at the pace I wanted. I had no control, but intuitively knew that it was only my ego stopping the very thing I needed to be happy. In time I would have pushed forward again, but the sense of loss, waste of time and missed experiences weighed down my soul.

Today, I feel none of this. I have the same concerns, but without having to defend my ego, I have the energy to look objectively at these issues. Where I had energy to fight off the ice storm's capacity to assimilate me, the insidious needs of the train had defeated me and I had accepted its goals as my own. Over the next weeks, with winter hurtling by, the speed of the train attempts to dictate the speed of my life. Everyday I am expected to race, only to rise the next day like an automaton and race again. Not only are the train's goals expected to be mine, but also its destination—the end of the year.

I look at the calendar and feel shame at the days I have crossed off waiting for the final station. This I vow to change.

I now take responsibility when life becomes blurred. Blaming the conductors – or, worse, the inanimate train itself— does nothing for my life. If I slow the pace of my life it becomes clearer and more defined. I may not always be able to stop the dominoes from falling, but I can dictate how quickly they fall. I will at least be aware of the ego's trap, know when I am falling back into old ways. This gives me choice. Slowing my life allows me to invoke the power of choice. I can choose to have purpose in my life, and I realize that I have been trying to look good, rather than actually be good.

I will take the time to have a second cup of coffee, or stop on the way home from work to remember my dad. These choices no longer last in lengths of time but are moments unto themselves. They are all lived in the now. I smile thinking of Dad telling me to "Look up." I think of keeping my chin up. My life is beginning to have meaning.

My dad would teach me to "Experience all of it, understand why you feel what you feel. Use this to strengthen yourself, not to harden yourself." He was teaching me not to just survive, but to grow beyond simple survival and always reach high—not to just try to look good, but to actually be good. I smile now, knowing that I will push through. The deeper I get into the season of winter, the more energy and control I experience. The speeding train, out of touch conductors, and blurred images will no longer be my way.

One day between classes I have a quiet moment, and stay at my desk while students stream in and out. I recall one of the innumerable games of catch that Dad and I used to have. When I was young, we enjoyed these games as much as any father and son. One beautiful summer day we ended the game and headed home. While walking along, he asked me about school and how I was doing, encouraging me to talk so that he knew his son, just the type of thing all great fathers do. Upon arriving home, I took our ball gloves and put them away. He called me back and uttered the most unexpected comment I had ever heard in my life. "If you ever do that again we will never play catch again."

My jaw dropped, I could not imagine what transgression I had committed for the ultimate penalty to be invoked. "What did I do wrong?" I stammered.

He quietly spoke. "You didn't say, thank you."

I quietly answered. "Sorry, Dad. Thanks." Years later, while sitting in my class, I ponder why Dad had been so severe with me. Taking a moment today, the answer quietly comes. It was his way to help me be aware. He demonstrated that he wanted, even expected, me to think all the time. He was telling me to be conscious.

It took only a moment in the middle of my typically busy day to figure this out, but it only happened because I did take that moment. I had puzzled on that exchange all my life. As soon as I slowed my life, took control of myself, became conscious, I instantaneously learned the lesson that my father was trying to teach all those years ago.

On the weekend, I ask my family if they would indulge me. I opt out of the family routines and spend most of the weekend lost in thought. I make the most of this time and out of respect for my family, work hard trying to understand a concept that is slowly becoming precious to me: consciousness. It means many vibrant and subtle things—objectivity, honesty and concentration among them.

I watch the last of the beautiful white snow disappear as winter weakens. The best it can offer is a strong rain. In the first serious run of the season, I come to a realization; if I am going to understand consciousness, I will have to understand dread. Since before school began this year, I have known dread as a companion. It is time to look and see it for what it is. To do this, I have the foreboding feeling that at some point, it will entail embracing dread.

After my run I am exhausted, and see that the long road back to running-shape lies before me. The rain has stopped, and before going in I notice that the moon has risen. Catching my breath and stretching, I see a long narrow cloud slowly cross the face of the full moon. That is what dread looks like. First there is your life, and then dread blows across it, then one's life returns. Dread does not change one's life. It filters through, setting the stage for choice. I smile when the full shine of the moon returns. I wonder if this is something every human experiences, something that we all have to encounter, alone.

I have been looking at dread all wrong. Dread only promotes change; it is neither good nor bad. Dread is whatever we make it. Before hitting the shower, I run to the dictionary to look up the meaning of dread. This is something I do often, as I have a deep respect for root words and defined meanings. The history of a word gives intense insight into our elders and the wise ones of past generations. Looking up dread I read: "Look forward to with fear or extreme unease or reluctance; fear greatly; regard with awe, fear of something that may or may not happen," and finally, "awe-inspiring."

I recall an old friend whom I have not thought of in years. We were in our early twenties and had shared all the life-adventures that males rushing to true manhood experience, at least their naïve version of manhood. One day, I pulled up beside him on the street and he uttered, to my shock, "I just dread seeing you." For years, I felt these were some of the heavier stones I carried.

Now I realize that many of our conversations forewarned of change. He was on the verge of a commitment that would change his life, and I was in a small way involved in that process. The dread he was feeling was much like the dread I have been dealing with. It was candidly acknowledging the internal struggle that gave birth to change. Now I can take those stones I have been carrying all these years, and leave them behind.

Monday morning comes, and with it the responsibilities of work. As always, I do not leave without hugging my family and then sharing how much I love them. I also say, "Thanks, for giving me some time to think this weekend. It helped tremendously." I also thought of Dad, the Scottish teacher, and my friend from the past. I had learned so much from all of them this weekend. Sometimes, exchanges from the past are like hidden wonders waiting to be discovered; we just have to take the time. What does not accompany me this Monday is fatigue and fear. Oddly, dread and I continue to coexist, but I am no longer reacting in fear. I have embraced it and accepted dread as part of me, part of my journey. It feels strangely reassuring to know that it is still near.

I start my workday by telephoning to see if Penny is going to attend my class. I have been doing this occasionally, not trying to harass, but just letting her know that I notice. Whenever I call, I am never able to converse with her directly. I only get the impersonal machine. All I ever say is, "It would be nice to see you and I hope you are okay." It is the most sincere thought I can express.

Her third period class arrives and I check her desk once again, but as usual, there is only an empty seat. Her potential has not left, but where she could have been sitting is just an empty space. With winter in its last throes, I wonder where she is. More importantly, I wonder how she is. Has she dropped out or, worse, been lost to the needle? I leave my class working on an assignment and search out the Scottish teacher. In this short walk across the hall I wonder if I am in the right profession, or is that just dread slinking behind me in search of my shadow. Before knocking on his classroom door, I remind myself that dread is nothing but a portal to change, I will embrace it... welcome it.

I apologize for interrupting his class and ask if he had seen Penny? His eyes smile as he says, "That's the first time you have ever asked about her. She has missed a couple of my classes, but generally, she attends. I know she makes it when she can." He pauses and seems to contemplate something and then adds, "I'm glad you're searching for her."

I ask, "Do you know why she isn't here, or what she is up to?"

His reaction reminds me of the cloud passing over the face of the moon. It is the first time I ever see him solemn. "Sorry. You'll have to ask her that." His answer does not alleviate my concern for the needle. I feel I have crossed an invisible barrier, or worse, encroached on a sacred trust. I walk back to my class wondering what it is that dread is trying to forewarn me about. If I keep searching, will I find that Penny is on the needle? Is dread trying to prepare me for this? Over the loudspeaker the conductor of the train announces, "For those of you who haven't noticed, tomorrow is the first day of spring."

I walk back into my class knowing dread may win the day, and I actually question again if the pain I am feeling means I am in the wrong profession. My emotions fluctuate from confidence to questioning the cornerstones of my life. Psychologically, I have been plowed into fertile ground for change.

Upon entering my class, I am too tired to deal with the noisy students who are out of their seats. Inwardly I feel panic. I have consciousness, I have choice, but fear is again beginning to paralyze me. Fatigue is returning and I feel the dominoes starting to fall. Change is happening, but not the change I want.

The students see me and awkwardly wait for me to chastise them. When I do not they slowly begin to sit with questioning expressions. Despite my fatigue, I notice behind them in the once empty seat a shadow that appears like a shape. I feel the muscles in my face involuntarily tensing as I realize this shadow has substance. My face breaks into a grin. Penny is sitting in her desk, quietly avoiding my eyes! I feel the way the moon feels when the last of the cloud passes, allowing it to see clearly again. Dread washes over me and I feel the changes

I want in my life begin again. I instantly know I am prepared for this. Thank you dread, thank you very much. In so many ways, the cold hard winter is over.

Epiphany: A sudden intuitive leap of understanding, especially through an ordinary but striking occurrence.

A stupid man tries to change the world.
A naïve man tries to change those around him.
A wise man tries to change himself.
~Unknown

Chapter 19

**The only way to make sense out of change is to
plunge into it, move with it, and join the dance.**
~Alan Watts

With the first day of the vernal season comes the traditional
hunting of the winter champagne cork. Whoever discovers the
whereabouts of the cork has the responsibility of picking the
evening wines. We have been doing this for a number of years,
and it feels right to acknowledge the seasons in this way. It is
just pagan enough to meet our needs.

If not for this ritual, it would have been difficult to know
that spring had sprung. Every day is cloudy, cool, and foggy,
misting too heavily to be called a spring shower. In this part of
the country, the seasons are usually distinct. Having day after
day of bleak gray conditions, neither winter cold nor blooming
spring is going to cause many neighbors to have cabin fever.

At work the effects of the weather are tangible. Tempers
are short and everyone—other than predictably the Scottish
teacher, and strangely Penny—is affected by the dreary conditions. I notice her attendance is irregular, although improved.
Our communication, sadly, remains infrequent. Despite this,
whenever I see her I say hello, and whenever she is absent I call

and say that I miss her. She rarely makes eye contact, but when she does we acknowledge each other for slightly longer periods each time.

In the staff room talk revolves around "The dog days." This baseball term describes the section of the schedule just beyond the halfway point, when players are tired and cannot see the end. In past years, I fought off these days by pretending that the school year was just beginning. By doing this I improve my patience, as well as help with the train ride. Often I wish my colleagues would learn this trick. Interestingly, this year I no longer pretend, as my patience for students and colleagues genuinely has improved. Just possibly, there are now three of us unaffected by the constant gray.

Lunch, as usual, is frantic and followed by heartburn. It always includes returning parent calls, telephoning absent students, and marking. It also means gym supervision, meetings, answering innumerable students' questions, hall supervision, and catching up students on missed assignments. As with professional cyclists in the Tour de France, the ability to eat in less than one minute, while moving at full speed, is a basic skill.

It is during one of these days when I have a fortuitous meeting with a student. While trying to get across a crowded hallway I notice movement under the stairs. It is such a dark and isolated hiding place I do not know how I even noticed him. It turns out to be the student who previously talked about suicide.

With students streaming up and down, I clamber under the stairs and ask if everything is okay. The boy-troll tells me that he is fine, a little embarrassed at his discovery, but fine. This is his place to come and be alone. I sit crossed-legged in the cramped confines, with only a little light from the hall illuminating us, and tell him that I understand. I ask how he is doing, sadly realizing that after I had taken him to the counselor, I had never bothered to ask this question. Sitting in the dark corner of the school, I feel deep shame that I have not followed up. I apologize for not checking on him and he looks at me oddly. Then suddenly, he breaks into an enormous grin. I am shocked at how little it takes to impact him. All I said was, "I'm sorry, I should have found you the next day and asked how you were doing." That's all it took.

From our hideout, we hear the hum of the train as it hurtles towards its destination. Curiously, we also hear the rain falling in the courtyard garden. Students smoking outside have left the door open at the end of the hall. They are breaking a school rule by smoking outside the designated "pit." My fellow troll asks if I am going to "bust them." He secretly enjoys being on the inside of this decision.

His face mirrors my surprise as I answer "No." For both of us, surprise turns to pride as I add, "What we're talking about is more important." It is then that his expression tells me he is going to share something personal.

He asks, "Do you know why I eat my lunch hidden away?" Not waiting for a response he continues, "The quiet slows down my life. The noise of this school doesn't allow me to deal with the things I need to think about." His Shadow is dancing the same dance that mine had. He continues sharing: "By being here, I feel in control and calm. It makes me confident that I'll never again consider suicide."

By choosing not to deal with the smokers, I have ignored my professional responsibilities. Only a season or two earlier I would have ignored *The Moment,* and done my job. Deciding to stay allows for something far more important to happen. In reality, by ignoring the rules of the train, its streaking journey slows for one lone passenger. He feels acknowledged.

I surprise him when I pull out my sandwich and, without saying a word, sit under the stairs with him and eat. During this lunch, I actually dialogue with one student, sharing that I also am trying to slow the pace of my life. He seems fascinated that someone my age is experiencing exactly what he is. His chest puffs with pride. I am having a direct and profound impact on the human being that is sitting in front of me. I had almost forgotten what that was like.

Far too early, the train's whistle screams "MOVE!" and students in mid-stride turn and head to class. I have not made it to the staff room or dealt with the smokers, nor does it matter. A student and I have connected on a very real and human level. It has been a long time since I have taken the time to do that.

While strolling to class with my hands in my pocket, I chuckle at a thought. A hundred years ago, kids would have been out in the back of the one-room schoolhouse, smoking. A hundred years from now, students will be smoking behind the monolith they call school. But both a hundred years ago, and a hundred years into the future, there is also a student desperate to talk to a teacher. I am proud of my choice.

My fellow troll and I make a commitment that once a week we will meet and, "Slow ourselves." This, we agree, will ensure that the train is not forcing us to live a pace that is not in our interest. For the rest of the year we keep our pact, meeting under the stairs while the train roars past. Not once, despite the train's schedule, does either one of us miss our luncheon meeting. During these encounters, we discuss everything from atomic energy to zoology. These meetings are as important to me as they are to him.

After thirty-three consecutive days of gray, one morning—while at my desk marking piles of exams—I see the unfathomable. A sunbeam reflects off the test papers hiding my desk. The calendar may show that we are a month into spring, but the spirit of winter has fought hard.

This moment of spring reminds me of the lotus blossom, so beautifully conceptualized in Buddhism. Where the light strikes my desk, I envision the lotus being coaxed open by spring's eternal hope. I imagine the blossom opening in day and closing each night, only to open again the next day. This thought compels me to compare it with hope and dread, dread and hope, two sides of the same coin.

My thinking is interrupted when my fellow troll pops his head into the class and asks, "Will we be meeting today?"

"What should our topic be?"

"Baseball cards," he says as he leaves. While leaning back in my chair, smiling, I place my hands behind my head and lace my fingers together. Is there a surer sign of spring than baseball? The little sunbeam breaks through the gray and fills my room with warm gold. While the train's chaos swirls about, I am content.

Just then the Scottish teacher enters and chuckles. "You look rather relaxed."

For no other reason than I had finally earned the right I look at him and ask, "I need you to be my mentor. Will you consider it?"

For some unfathomable reason this brings a doubled over belly-laugh from him. Once he regains control and wipes tears of laughter from his eyes he answers, "I always have been." As usual, I am confused as he adds, "All counseling, all mentoring, all relationships come down to one person helping the other to answer two questions. Do you know what those questions are?"

I smile with realization, "Who are you, and what do you believe in?"

"Yes," he smiles, "I started you on that road when I asked, why are you a teacher and what gives you the right? You have answered these questions, have you not?"

"I have."

"So allow me to share a story. A person has two wands. One touch from the first wand gives you everything you want: money, security, even health, all the things most humans think they want. The other wand can only offer one thing, peace! And even that will last for only a moment—a single, brief moment of peace. All of humanity appears to pursue the first wand. But, conscious people, they search for the second wand." He adds, "The frustration that humanity feels is because they are subconsciously aware that they spend their life searching for the wrong wand. Even one moment of peace brings more consciousness than a lifetime with wealth and security."

I ask, "Surely health is more important than a fleeting moment of peace?"

"Not so," he answers. "Ask a dying patient which he would want, his health back or simple peace. We both know that if he is conscious he will choose peace. What good is health if you have no peace? Yet if you have peace and are dying from cancer, you have all that you need."

Sunshine bursts into my classroom and floods it in bright light. Surely a coincidence.

Chapter 20

If you follow your bliss, you put yourself on a kind of track, which has been there all the while waiting for you, and the life that you ought to be living is the one you are living.
~Joseph Campbell

I wake to the smell of freshly-cut grass permeating our bedroom. With it comes the olfactory memory of baseball. The kids wake early, and are enthusiastically doing their chores—or so I imagine as I lie in bed.

I had promised that on the first warm weekend we would all hike down "Cardiac Hill" to the beach. Once I roust myself out of bed, we are out the door by mid-afternoon.

While playing in the sand, we see a remarkable sight. Lab misses most of the incident, as he is oblivious to everything but the shore birds. Using his aerodynamic training, he pins back his ears and races up and down the beach chasing seagulls off his private playground. It is clear that he is taking it as a personal affront every time a bird rests.

A seal is enjoying a morning meal of fish while basking on a swimmer's float, when, suddenly, a bald eagle falls out of a tree and unfolds its huge wings. He swoops low over the beach toward the bay; once his flight path is determined he is never higher than two feet above the water. His destination becomes clear as he heads toward the seal like a guided missile. Not once does he beat his wings, as any movement would give away his position. The stealth eagle gets within ten feet of the lounging seal and is still unnoticed other than by my family. He times his theft so that the raft will rise on a wave and he can actually attack from slightly below. With final flight path calculated, he judges his arrival perfectly—except for one unseen, slightly larger, rogue wave.

The raft bobs infinitesimally higher than the eagle calculated and the swell causes one of those uncoordinated moments of nature most humans never see. The eagle is cutting through the sea air too quickly to adjust and his unfolded talons rap on the wooden raft startling the seal. The impact jerks the eagle awkwardly forward, and the seal reacts by sitting up and dropping his fish. In this fluttering, distinctly un-eagle-like position he smacks the shocked seal fully chest to chest. The impact is heard back the one hundred meters to where we stand with our mouths agape.

The seal immediately dives into the water and the eagle flies awkwardly back to the tree, talons empty. He flutters directly over me and his proud white head is slightly flushed with embarrassment.

Meanwhile, Lab is barking frantically and all his formidable concentration is focused laser-like on one particular seagull. One of Jonathon Livingston's children circles lazily then casually lands on the now abandoned raft. He gobbles the remaining fish at his leisure, disturbed by neither seal nor eagle.

Lab is devastated at his mortal adversary's success—until a crab distracts him and, nose-down, off he sniffs. The crab scurries between his legs, which makes Lab lose all control of his feet, let alone his dignity. He runs down the beach on his hind legs, with front paws flailing. The crab makes for the water and arrives easily as Lab, after realizing that he can't run on two legs, turns himself almost inside out, trying to figure out where his adversary has gone. Realizing the crab has escaped, he follows his scent into the water where the horrible reality dawns upon him. His paws are getting wet!

Sadly, Lab suffers from the debilitating dog disorder called wet paw syndrome. He reverses his four-wheel drive and frantically back peddles to dry land. Poor Lab is cautiously examining his wet feet when suddenly his eyes bulge. A new playmate, a clam geyser, catches his eye. Feet forgotten, he stalks the sandy beach watching for the little geysers to squirt into the air.

I sit amazed, watching the life that dog has.

At the end of the day we are all exhausted. The two-mile downhill stroll becomes a death march when ascending on the way home. I have run "Cardiac" hundreds if not thousands of times. However, after hours of turning over rocks on the beach and listening to the squeals of delight emanating from my children, walking home is somehow more difficult than running. It may be all the pails, shells, and blankets I have to carry that, upon nearing the apex, forces my nose to the asphalt.

Once home, my family's heads are filled with wonderful memories of the day. The sun is giving off the last of its golden rays as dusk breaths its last light. Lab curls with my family on our deck. He licks his feet as if to ask, "When did these get wet?"

The day has one last memory to reveal before the kids trudge off to dreamland. I am watering our garden when we see the first hummingbird of the season. When the sun hits it just right, it darts about like an orange orb. At first, I think it is avoiding the shower of water sprinkling from my hose. Then my wife laughs, "It wants a bath." I hold my thumb over the nozzle, creating an artificial spring drizzle, and the humming-bird maneuvers into its center. It hovers there enjoying the not so private shower. The water drops reflect the light, so it appears like a brilliantly florescent spinning top dangling in the air. My kids have one last squeal of delight before accepting the inevitability of bedtime. Off to bed they march with humming-birds dancing in their heads.

I contemplate how substantive this day is for me. I have come to the realization that in life I have choices. I can look for, and if lucky, find my bliss, or ignore that such a thing exists. Because I have earned it, time runs slower now and I have more energy. From a place deep within, I ponder the lotus blossom. I must bring to my mentor a question. "Is the lotus blossom actualizing its bliss with every morning incarnation?" I am curious what his answer will be.

The next morning recreates the smells of the previous day: pure baseball. I organize a backpack with food and water for the family's hike up the neighborhood mountain.

The trail is safe but steep, so there is little talking as each of us is having an intense internal monologue. With few words spoken, I assume that the kids are thinking about their upcoming baseball tryouts. My wife is remembering that each year the first time up this trail is the hardest. We all know what is going on in Lab's head: "I should have brought my bowl. Oh, a squirrel! Next time I'll bring my bowl. Oh a slug! Why didn't I bring my bowl...?"

My thoughts drift to the little troll and our weekly meetings under the stairs. I feel good about slowing the train and not allowing its speed to dictate what is going to happen. In a small way, I am learning how to help a passenger step off the train, deal with what needs to be dealt with and then get back aboard without being left behind. It is invigorating to care about someone else.

Resting, I realize that even this little trail is one of the paths of my life. This scraped trail has been here for over a thousand years, used by man and animal alike. When my kids come around the corner, following Mom and a panting Lab, I experience true bliss. I can see that for miles in every direction it is clear, and my companion dread is nowhere near.

Reaching the crest, we collapse, ready for lunch. From the summit, we look across the harbor at the mountain trails upon which I am again running. Between bites we look down on our beautiful world, and know that we live in one of the most spectacular places on the planet. I wander away to find a quiet rock seat facing south. From here, I can look for as far as my vision allows. Numerous islands peek defiantly out of the ocean. I do not know if it is the quiet or my sense of bliss, but I am in harmony with my surroundings. Maybe it is because I sit in the middle of an old aboriginal, "medicine wheel", but reality fills me. Is this what fully conscious people experience? How amazing it would be to meander through one's life in this state. My mentor has mentioned that when he retires he prefers no party. On his last day, he wants to simply wander out the door and walk into his sunset. When I first heard this I thought it strange, but now I understand.

My state of bliss is interrupted by an unusual noise. In my life, I have had many encounters with bears, so whenever I hike, I am hypersensitive to the possibility of meeting one. On more than one occasion, this alertness has prevented me from stumbling into a dangerous situation. Predictably, the noise is directly behind me. I look slowly to see if Lab is rummaging, but see that he has found shade near the family. I concentrate, and am sure a large animal is just behind me. Turning slowly, my eyes strain peripherally, but to no avail. If I am upwind, I have a good chance of seeing him before he sees me. I will be able to devise a strategy of sitting still, slowly backing away, or—my least favorite—running in the opposite direction of my family to draw him away. Again, I turn slowly and see nothing. Sitting still, I hear the noise again and know it is close. The sound shifts to my left then with remarkable agility it moves to my right, while always remaining close. Astonishingly, it is not a bear foraging, but a dragonfly!

It is so quiet up here that a dragonfly's wing, in close proximity to my ears, sounds out of proportion. I relax and watch the battleship-blue-gray tinted miniature dragon manipulate its amazing combination of wings. I am very glad that I did not overreact, and had saved myself the humiliation of sprinting past my family in a panic yelling, "Bear! Bear!" The dragonfly flutters off like a helicopter with a rotor problem.

A warm breeze flits among the trees and the sound is amplified. Smells flow through me and I am one with the moment. Of all the seasons, spring is the most balanced. Everything is in harmony. An hour or two before sunset, the flying insects take to the air in little tornadoes. Dusk brings out the darting feeders, dragonflies and hummingbirds. At sunset they quickly skedaddle as the big boys, swallows and nighthawks, hunt. Then finally, in the dark come the night raiders: bats. Every night the synchronism is perfect.

Sitting in my own medicine-wheel, built nearly a thousand years ago, I realize dragonflies and baseball are the same thing. The seasons—baseball, bugs, dragonflies, swallows, bats, lotus blossoms – are all about rebirth. Everything begins again. Spring, more than any other season, brings choice.

The dragonfly taught me that an opportunity to learn sits untiringly beside us every conscious moment. The prospect of attaining bliss is waiting in the sound of a dragonfly's wings or under the stairs of a school. Just like the potential that sits patiently waiting for each child, bliss is equally vigilant whenever the opportunity for choice arises. In Spring's bloom germinates the seed of evolution, enabling us to "spring" forward and be reborn.

The lessons that I must learn to evolve are always available. They are everywhere; I only have to be aware and determined to learn. Free will does not dictate if the opportunity is available or not. Free will simply exercises the choice to either seize the occasion or squander it. The moments that make up our life exist for us to decide; do we choose to evolve or not? That is the deeper meaning of my second epiphany. Life is an opportunity to learn the lessons in order to evolve. My lessons may be different from every other person's, but their lessons also wait eternally.

The Tao to evolution's blossoming is consciousness. To evolve we must be conscious. The consummation of that consciousness is bliss. It simply waits indefatigably for whomever wants it. While we struggle with dread and ego, shadows and angst, we sometimes forget that the lotus is perfect long before it blooms.

Chapter 21

When you work you are a flute through whose heart the whispering of the hours turns to music. To love life through labor is to be intimate with life's inmost secret. All work is empty save when there is love, for work is love made visible.
~Kahlil Gibran

Recently, I have become aware that each workday is the same as the previous. It begins with a spectacular vista of opportunity. Miraculously, the days now end the same way. I stand outside my class to greet students before the annoying squeal of the train's whistle. When students enter, I make eye contact and say "hello"—all in the name of acknowledging passengers, especially those barely holding on.

My "Hello, Brenda" or "Good to see you, Brian," are met with varying degrees of shrugs. There is the uncomplicated single shoulder shrug that gives the impression of a door slamming shut. The more complicated, yet surprisingly popular, simultaneous double-shoulder shrug imitates a substantial rock wall. Sophisticated double shoulder shrugs, done separately, first one shoulder and then the other, gives the perception of bricks laid one on top of the other. Finally, some of the more jaded of the train's passengers use a combination, an elaborate form of the simultaneous double-shoulder shrug that includes arms slightly bent at the elbow, palms up and head tilted to the side. This is always accompanied by a mumbled, "Whatever." This maneuver I call, "The Fortress."

However, none of their efforts deter me, as I choose to be recognized and I will accomplish this by acknowledging them. We exist, and the first step is to say "Hi." This is my choice. Being ignored is no longer acceptable. Besides, my effort gives them identity.

Only two students do not resort to the shoulder shrug defense. One is my troll-lunch partner, who recently went to his counselor requesting a transfer into my class. From him I get a big, "Hi" and eye contact. This is no small event in my life. The other student is, surprisingly, Penny. She does not yet accept my greetings but has devised a unique defense. Instead of using her shoulders, she drops her head infinitesimally, avoiding my eyes. In turn, I make it my personal mission to greet her every-day. My efforts continue day after day.

In time, a few passengers respond with begrudging grunts. Over days, then weeks, this progresses to "Hi," and "Hey." Later, we add small things like, "How are you?" and on a good day, "How was your last class?" Penny never says any-thing, but sometimes I choose to believe that her head lowers a little less than other days. I take my successes wherever I can find them. Everyday I go home happy.

One night I am curious, and work up the courage to ask my wife, "During the winter, do you remember telling me you liked the look on my face."

"Of course I do."

My courage hangs tough, so I continue. "Have you seen it lately?"

Her response is a resounding, "All the time, but better. It's not just a look. You act lighter, and it shows in your body language. It's as if you're not taking everything so seriously." Then she adds gold. "Your journey suits you."

"Thanks. It feels like I'm growing. I have chosen to leave many rocks by the side of the road. I feel more in control, and have more choices. It's funny."

"How so?"

"Every instinct I have tells me I am just beginning, and that there is so much more."

What she says next enters my consciousness unconditionally: "If there is more to come, I want to explore it with you. I know that whatever happens to you happens to me."

Once again, it is clear that I have so much. This time, however, I not only feel it but also realize for the first time; I have so much... to give!

The next day, on the way to work, I pull over to observe the spectacular mating dance of hummingbirds. The morning sun catches the florescent feathers of the males as they soar high into the morning air, only to take a dramatic dive in an effort to impress the rather drably dressed females. The strutting orbs dash about at neck-wrenching speeds. The gathering grows in numbers as word magically passes down the valley. I can only stay a moment, but it is a moment I will remember forever—not for any spectacular reason, but for the everydayness of the scene and because I simply do not miss the now.

Pulling into the school parking lot, I fixate my mind on the display of hummingbirds. I walk into the courtyard where stress usually waits. Every day it sits on the school bench beside a small garden. We then walk together from here to my classroom. Not today, however! For the first time, I notice a pleasant odor, so I luxuriate in the fine spring smell. I will never know if they have just blossomed or have always been there, but between the cement walk and brick wall are small bushes of wild roses.

As I admire them a sense, or voice, something, tells me to look up. High in a third floor window Penny stands watching. When she notices that I see her, she turns away. This time, I am certain there is a smile on her face—well, at least a wry angle at the corners of her mouth. Maybe it's a smirk, or just a stoned grin. No, I am sure it is a smile. I will take my successes where I can.

At lunch today, my student-troll decides the discussion on baseball will continue. Under the stairs he explains. "This game is the only one not ruled by time. Outs, the game itself, dictates when it ends. There are no periods, quarters, or half times that ruin the perfect symmetry that is baseball." This conversation encourages him to share that he is having difficulty at school, and is thinking he might quit so that his problems do not overwhelm him again. The speed of the train is getting to be too much.

I share a story about Cal Ripken's baseball career. "Cal appears to play one inning at a time and each inning becomes a game, which merges into a season. Eventually the seasons grows into "The Streak." This evolves into his career, a career that transcends the game, one inning at a time, one long inning of excellence and effort." The train slows. My student understands, and promises that he will take it one class at a time. I love my job.

Lunch ends, and half the students I greet continue to throw up shoulder-shrug walls and one even persists with the impenetrable "Fortress." Penny is unrelenting with her eyes cast down and silence upon entering the room. But she enters!

Just before closing the door, I catch the eye of my mentor. He is across the hall at his desk, just watching. He gives me thumbs up and I return the gesture. The message is understood. When we find time, we will talk.

Driving home after work, I stop by the lakes and listen for my favorite spring sound. The sun is sharing its last rays and the air holds the perfume smell of this morning, when on cue, I hear her. She circles the lake making music for her mate. In the country, only the wolf's howl can match the soul-searching timbre of a loon. The loon's cry touches my soul, and I acknowledge that I not only love my wife, but have also fallen deeply in love with my life.

Chapter 22

It is characteristic of the ego that it takes all
that is unimportant as important and all that
is important as unimportant.
~Meher Baba

The light reaches my consciousness despite the fact that my eye-
lids are still one with sleep. Flashbulbs explode in our bedroom.
Once fully awake, I see that the night view out the skylight
reveals a silent lightning storm. I watch as sheet-lightning
exposes the horizon. Eventually, far in the distance, a roll of
thunder turns into a thunderclap as it boils over the water preparing to unleash itself on the harbor. The windows of our log
home appear to bend with the concussion sent from an ancient
Viking God.

My legs are still numb with sleep when I hear the predictable sound that always follows thunder. I ask my legs to
respond and they say, maybe. I hustle, the best I can, to comfort
poor Lab. He is inside, but the sound of his bowl dropping in
panic on the concrete greets me as I open the basement door.
Before I can react, he leaps past me up the "No dogs allowed"
stairs. He bounds all the way to the forbidden loft. By the time
I make it up to the lair of my castle, Lab is cowering under the

sheets with my giggling wife. I climb back into bed, shove him over and drop my head back onto my pillow. There is a loud clunk, and I feel something like a brick in my pillowcase. Lifting my pillow reveals the obvious; Lab has scooped up his bowl from the basement, and brought it with him. I respectfully place it next to him. The storm lasts an hour, as does our consoling of Lab. By the time he regains his composure, the storm has softened into a gentle spring shower. The soft morning rain, in anticipation of the afternoon sunshine, wipes clean everything in the harbor.

Other than me, all living creatures under the protection of our log home decide to sleep in. The sound and smell of this morning makes me think not of common everyday rain but of falling dew. Sitting under the porch's roof, it is easy to imagine the entire world being cleansed. While the soft dew falls, I consider how much I have changed. What was important to me, only fleeting months ago, no longer has any value.

My core has evolved. If a person can change at the sub-atomic level, I have. I am now an evolving entity, not a stagnate being. I'm like a baby who has just discovered knees and elbows, and can't wait to use them. Only for me, it is eyes and ears: I am seeing and hearing for the very first time. With this insight comes the responsibility to use them.

As life begins stirring in my home, another revelation arrives. Just as dread is a part of losing one's shadow, becoming conscious is a process of moving past a point in life that has already forgotten me. Where my shadow once existed, I had not. In many ways it is as if I have never been there. The perspectives that I now hold dear are influenced by the questions that my mentor raised during our time together. I have often wondered how he found the energy, let alone the time, to meditate on such weighty subjects.

As of this moment, I can now choose what is important.

I understand why he asks such difficult questions. I now have both the energy and time to contemplate... simply because it is important to me.

It is an odd culture that has taken its population from "How can I help you?" to "What have you done for me lately?" The sense of entitlement that attaches to this type of thinking represents the shattering of a society.

I gave my dozing family hugs before leaving for school. Despite the lack of sleep, due mainly to the personal nocturnal habits of Lab, the twitching legs and some rather odious doggy odors, it is good to go to work. I am actually energized.

On the drive to work I avoid the empty canoes that change lanes for a ten second advantage. My classes go well, and in the hallway the principal surprisingly calls my name. He races through the hall and stops, out of breath. He blurts out a few words and then frantically speeds off. Some people admire how hard he works, but I am not a fan of the frenzied tone it sets. To me, it adds to the chaos and stress of an unhealthy educational atmosphere. However, for a train with only one destination in mind, it is a very appropriate pace.

I can only guess at the words spewed since they came at me faster than the speed of sound. Working with about every third word, I interpret a compliment. I could make out the words "work, noticed, excellent" and something that sounded like "keep going," but I will never know for sure. Reflecting back, I am sure the words "good" and, "year" were also ejaculated. I would like to appreciate what he is trying to do, but it is all said at a decibel level so high that maybe only Lab could interpret. I simply have no context upon which to hang his comments, and refuse to accept mediocrity as the standard. These rock chips and fragments will be left at the side of the freeway.

Standing still in the speedway used by the train's passengers, I apparently stand out, with possibly an odd expression

145

on my face. I notice two people intently watching me. At one end of the hall, standing rock still while passengers race about, is my mentor. The administrator rapidly closes the distance to him, says something, then abruptly brushes past and is gone. My mentor does not acknowledge him but instead continues to stare. His eyes leave me and look down the hall. I follow his gaze. At the opposite end of the hall, standing rock still, is Penny. I look back at my mentor who slowly turns and disappears down an adjacent hallway. This is peculiar.

My eyes return to Penny who is focused laser-like on me. When we make eye contact, she too turns slowly and vanishes down a side passage. A shiver of confusion runs down my spine.

What stands out is that they both appear to move in slow motion. Chaos envelopes both, but it does not seem to touch them. I can understand my mentor appearing to move slower than those around him, as that would be just like him, to set his own pace. My only explanation for Penny's slow movement is that she is stoned.

Coincidentally, the next class is Penny's. I want to arrive ahead of her, so I cut across the courtyard. Time speeds up. The rose perfume still hangs in the air, and despite my mission I notice it. I arrive first and take a few deep breaths, so that I appear calm while welcoming my students. When she enters I say, "Nice to see you today." My new consciousness may make perceptions relative, but her reaction appears to be different. It no longer looks to me as if she lowers her head in shyness or stoned paranoia. It is as if she bows to me, a sign not of submission but of respect. Have I been misunderstanding her all this time?

I am seeing the same world, only the seasons have changed, but it all appears radically different. The time and energy I have been spending on myself now focuses on the world outside me, and that changes everything. The same cycle that drove me to frustration and fatigue is now working in reverse. My world had been small when my ego was big. Now with my ego small my universe is expanding. Maybe I really have misunderstood Penny's actions. This thought startles me.

During class, I decide that today is the day. When the whistle declares the end of class by screaming, "MOVE!" I ask Penny to wait. I prepare for her to drop her books right then and storm out. Behind her intelligent eyes, I can tell she is making a decision. She chooses, and sits in a desk. I extend the risk by saying, "I notice you haven't said much in class." She stares back. I continue. "I overheard you once explain about words being like rocks, so I have a small understanding why you are quiet." Her face shows little response, but if I see anything, she seems impressed. "I know you are struggling, but you can make it. I really want you to attend class."

She breaks her silence and hands me a boulder. "Why?"

I feel the weight of her word and try to respond with a nugget of gold. "I know... I'm surprised too... I'm slowly learning what teaching is all about."

I do not know if I've blown my chance as she calmly picks up her books and quietly stands. With only a quick glance she heads for the door. My heart sinks. At the door she stops and says, "You're going to make me think." With that, she leaves. The exchange leaves me numb since months of work just walked out the door, and I do not know what will happen next. Driving home, I am surprisingly pleased that despite our encounter I still have energy. I am at least trying.

After dinner, I ask the family who wants to walk around the lakes and watch the full moon rise. It feels great to want to do something after work. Only a few months ago, the stamina for a walk after my workday would have been out of the question. I am also proud that my entire family chooses to participate.

Beside one of our neighborhood lakes, we hear baby eaglets in full squawk. They make such a demanding and distinctive sound while waiting impatiently for food. From high above, the mother eagle dives. Soon the forest is silent as, in some unseen nest, babies are fed. I notice that Lab and our kids are standing perfectly still, a phenomenon unto itself. When my wife and I catch up, we peer into the rainforest that shelters the road. Ten feet into the green is an owl, watching us as intently as we are curious about it. It is a cute and rare sight to enjoy before turning toward home.

A faint glow reveals the heavenly promise of the coming full moon. The glow expands at the peak of the mountain guarding our harbor. The moonrise is quick, spectacular and memorable. It is so bright as it rises above the distant tree line that all the branches of the trees are revealed. For a moment, it almost looks as if trees grow on the moon. It moves higher, washing the stars from the night sky, then guides us home as clearly as if the sun was out. When we arrive, we tuck our kids and Lab into their beds and sit outside, watching the moon glitter silver on the harbor water. Sleep is restful that night.

The next day, Penny's class is first period. I am early, greeting students, but there is no sign of her. The whistle screams "MOVE!" as the train is about to jolt out of the station. I begin closing my door, and look down the empty hall and want to shout, "All aboard."

As I begin the day's lesson I think, "Damn. I blew it." Then suddenly, there is a quiet knock. Opening the door, I smile so my face beams. I am sure she notices, and I add, "Great to see you, Penny. Welcome." She mumbles nothing while her head dips as she enters. She is here, and since actions speak louder than words, I am victorious.

The class progresses like all first period classes. I am more like a dentist pulling teeth than an educator teaching.

With twenty minutes remaining in the period, I do something that I have never done before. I ask the students to close their books, put everything away and clear their desks. The students hesitantly do as I ask. They look as if I am asking them to remove a yoke from around their necks. Worse, a yoke they do not like but have grown accustomed to. There is trepidation in their movements, as if they are concerned that their familiar yoke will be replaced with a bigger one. In the back of the class I hear a student verbalize what is on everyone's mind. He says the unspeakable... the word most hated..."Test."

"No," I laugh. "I just want to take a moment and talk with you." One hundred percent of the faces looking back at me are skeptical. I share about my family's walk the previous night. I share about hearing the eagles and their babies. The girls collectively sigh when I tell them how the owl shyly peaked around the tree. I share how the moon lit our walk and encouraged them to "Check out the moon tonight."

The twenty minutes fly by and the whistle gently tells us to "MOVE!" to the next station. Passengers stream out, and they actually appear wider-awake than when they arrived. Penny walks past, and I try to make eye contact. I get more. She stops and quietly says, "I also saw that moon last night." She then quickly lowers her eyes and darts out. I choose not to say anything. We have connected, and besides, it is hard to speak with the smile that I have on my face. It is a good day.

During the break, I contemplate what is important to me and how it has changed. Today, I took my class off-task and time away from the mighty God Curriculum. I share something personal with a room of strangers. One student, Penny, has said seven words to me, and by doing so acknowledges both of us. We both now exist. I am amazed at what has become important to me.

Chapter 23

The attainment of enlightenment from the ego's point of view is extreme death.
~Chogyam Trungpa

Spring break arrives, and it cannot come at a better time. I am slowly becoming the "me" that I want to be – or at least something more than that formed in society's psyche.

One of my favorite activities is taking our canoe out onto the lakes, and paddling here and there with no specific destination in mind. Seeing my world from a different perspective is always refreshing. The best time to push off from shore is just before dusk, arriving in the middle of the lake a moment or two before the gloaming. While drifting about, I always watch for the running of the dandelions. The seeds look like miniature tumbleweeds sprinting over the calm lake. They race individually and in gangs, at amazing speeds, to unseen finish lines.

Once in the middle of the lake, I kneel in the center of the canoe, paddle resting across my lap, and just bob like a cork while the lights of shoreline cabins begin to twinkle. Starlight grows in strength, reflecting in the lake, and I am surrounded by absolute beauty.

I do this often and with all possible family combinations,

but secretly my favorite crew member is Lab. He wears an expression that is part, "Why am I in this contraption?" and "Woohoo! I'm having an adventure."

Tonight, however, I have the canoe to myself so I stargaze. I think back to when I finally found time to ask my mentor. "Is the lotus blossom actualizing its bliss with every morning incarnation?"

Surprisingly, he reacted as if it were an absolutely normal question. "Good teachers teach identity and provide opportunity. The rest is just details." At first, I did not understand, and he delighted in adding to my confusion. "A good teacher removes himself, thus creating a space for students to learn for themselves."

Completely lost, I had stammered, "What does that have to do with the lotus blossom?"

"Does the lotus blossom know that it is a lotus blossom?"

"I assume on some level. It at least knows that it is not a cat."

"Exactly. Lotus blossoms seldom act like cats."

That imagery made us laugh, and then I understood. The lotus blossom attains bliss with every morning incarnation because it knows that it is a lotus blossom.

Somehow, my mentor saw my understanding and concluded, "Exactly. Once a student knows who they are, they then have the opportunity to attain bliss. That is the moment the good teacher moves aside and allows his student to encounter whatever it is that he needs to experience."

With that, he 'moved aside' by getting into his car and driving off.

As the canoe rocks, my mind drifts to another incident. Just before canoeing, I was rearranging firewood, making room for three more cords, when I noticed a salamander had made its home among the dry and apparently safe wood. I carelessly moved his area of the condominium and unthinkingly shoved the woodpile over. Restacking it, I picked up a large piece of wood revealing the little guy lying motionless. I waited for him to scurry away, but his tail was unnaturally rigid and stood straight up, then slowly, very slowly, relaxed and lowered as life left. I watched, helpless, as he lost energy and was gone. His jet black eyes became death black. He died without a mark on his body.

It bothers me that my laziness, my unconsciousness, has caused a life to cease. I understand that things live, things die, and it is nature's way, but this salamander was there, and now it is gone.

Only with the stars can I share my shame. That perfect little salamander revealed simultaneously how far I have come and how far I have to travel. Sitting beside him as he died, all I had to offer was respect, and somehow that was not enough.

With the waves lapping against the canoe, I again hear my mentor's voice. "How would things be different if you weren't here?" I cannot tell if his voice rises from the lake or falls from the sky. I try to imagine a world without me. My realization is that there would be little difference between my death and the salamander's.

All that would remain of my time here is how I affected the people around me. That would really be the only difference between the salamander and me. Except for the people I affect, life would go on as if I was never here. My mentor's question is trying to teach me the importance of every person I meet.

Floating along, I am blissfully unaware that just ten minutes after entering the school tomorrow, his lesson will be taught again, in a much harsher way.

While walking through the school hallway I hear the announcement. "Would all staff please attend a meeting in the staff room. Immediately." Usually this means a practiced bureaucratic goodbye to a secretary or support staff, complete with a stale one-candle cake. One look at the administrator's face however, tells me that this occasion is far more serious. He breaks the news to us through tears and with voice cracking. One of the darkest aspects of the teaching profession is when a student dies. We listen in silence.

I hear her name, and hear that she has died, and all I can think about is the last time we talked. She is the ex-student who came to see me at the beginning of the school year, and shared that she was still doing drugs. I had no time for her then, because I was fulfilling the needs of the bureaucracy. I had truly believed that I would see her again. I wander through the day, thinking that I do not know if I could have helped her, but I do know that I could have tried. I had failed her. In that moment, the last of my ego dies an extreme death.

For the rest of the day, the staff carries out their duties in a fog. It is amazing how well behaved the students are once they sense, and later learn that tragedy has occurred. While watching staff and students deal with the day, my consciousness accepts that I must try to help whenever and whomever I can.

On the way home, I count the number of students that have left from the beginning of the year. It is only four, not an earth-shattering number, but what I realize next forces me to stop and reflect. Reality has a way of making one do that. I had not even tried to help any of the four students who left. This is intolerable. Two students in the first week left my class and never returned. Roughly six months ago, another student quit not only my class but also school. We never even said goodbye.

The fourth one had paid the final price: death. The girl I had been too busy dealing with paperwork to talk to now has an entire school mourning.

While steering my jeep back onto the highway, my mind shifts to Penny. I know that if she quits school it will be a loss to me, personally. Arriving home, I hug my wife and kids. The second thing I do is go into the backyard and find that salamander I had raked to a corner of the yard. I find a place on the side of a small hill, and respectfully bury it.

Before returning inside, I think of my mentor and his other question. "What are you doing with your time here?" Sorrow for a child who lost a most precious gift resounds within. With concentration and effort, I can be more. I can be conscious. I can have effect.

Before sleep comes that night, I acknowledge that a little piece of me has died. At some primal level in my life, I have been a victim—a victim not of society, or bureaucracy, or other people, but betrayed by my own ego. All this time, it has been tricking me—at times even controlling me. My ego's will had permeated every corner of my life. I had become one of "them," the "them" of whom I had so often complained. "They" are lazy, even unconscious, and now I realize... so was I. Laziness forces one to accept mediocrity. Lazy acceptance is the antichrist to consciousness.

I will now do everything I can, not only to prevent Penny from dropping out, but any other student. I will have time to talk to whoever wants to talk, and not allow myself to be manipulated by the situation. Everybody has his or her own lessons and journeys to experience. When something inside me died, I became closer to understanding what my mentor once said. "We are them until we decide not to be. It is just a conscious choice." I am beginning to understand.

Chapter 24

Never say there is nothing beautiful in the world anymore. There is always something to make you wonder, in the shape of a leaf, the trembling of a tree.
~Albert Schweitzer

The following days travel slowly as people come to terms with a former student's death. In class, students are sad and quiet. I worry about Penny as she slides back into missing classes. My concern for her involvement in drugs increases.

Suddenly, my mentor enters the staff room. A grim glare replaces his familiar jovial smile. The vice-principal and the counselor follow him into the room, both hurriedly explaining their point of view. All I hear is my mentor saying, "So you're just going to give up and let her go?" Uncomfortably and instantaneously, they all choose to go in separate directions.

Later, when the opportunity presents I ask, "What was the dark cloud in the staff room all about?"

My mentor's answer stabs my heart. "They're letting Penny go. They say her attendance has been so poor there isn't enough time for her to pass. She's going to get kicked out." Speechless, my brain tries to reject what it hears. He continues.

"They actually told her that she is not the right material for this school. Can you believe that?" Then he laughs.

"Why in the world are you laughing?"

"Apparently, when she left she asked: 'What material am I right for then?'"

My reaction is an overwhelming desire to call her and offer support. At the very least, if I stand beside her at this time I might provide some hope. It is the least I can do. I prepare my usual message for her answering machine when to my surprise Penny answers. "How are you?" I ask quickly. "I hear you were asked to leave school. I want to know if you're okay." The hope I have to offer is, "If you promise to attend my class everyday until the end of the year, I'll ask the principal to consider giving you a second chance." My offer is met with silence.

Finally the earpiece crackles. "Why would you do that?"

I hesitate before responding, finding the most honest answer I can. "I see the potential you have, and I want you to attain all that you can. To do this you need all the education you can get." I choose to go farther and risk the conversation's good will by adding, "I worry about you and drugs." An image of blood dripping from a dull needle swirls in my head.

"Drugs?" she queried.

"I saw you during Christmas and it is clear that you hang out with some heavy users. That and your poor attendance are sometimes signs of a dangerous lifestyle."

Her next words are ones that I do not expect. "Can I come and see you?"

"Yes. Absolutely. Anytime."

Before I leave work, Penny arrives. I have already talked to the principal and we have argued. How can he give up on any student if one staff member is still willing to try? To his credit he listens. She can stay as long as she comes everyday. To my great pleasure, Penny agrees to this. Later that day, my mentor walks up to me and silently shakes my hand.

On my drive home, all I think about is the drug world. What Penny revealed about her involvement in that world had an immense effect. She acknowledged that she hangs with drug users and consequently misses classes. When she shared this with me, my concern is reinforced... until she reveals that her work as a peer counselor at a drug center keeps her away from school. I almost fell over. It had never occurred to me.

The next day, I wait until last period to see if Penny will keep her word and attend. I hope and feel that she will, but as usual, she surprises me.

I walk early to my class, brimming with anticipation, when my mentor passes with an odd expression and mutters. "A little late for class aren't you?" Confused, I keep going and unlock my classroom door. I walk into a room that is not empty. Penny sits at her desk, and from the smile on her face I know that she asked my mentor to let her into the room early.

"Nice to see you," I stammer knowing that her actions are a sign of gratitude. It is then that she asks me never to share with anyone about her peer drug counseling. It is something that is personal and private. I agree and do not ask why. She seems to appreciate that. I believe that my mentor has the same agreement with her. That is why he could not tell me where she was when she missed classes, and that I would have to learn that from her. Neither my mentor nor I ever talk about this subject.

From the very beginning of her second chance, I am honest with her. She will have to work hard and even then, she might not pass. She is so far behind—but if we work together, it might happen. There are no shortcuts because that would be disrespectful to the other students, especially those who give their best effort and just pass. She agrees. When the final whistle screams that the train is stopping for the night, I give her extra homework. She smiles, but only after I explain that the harder she works, the more marking I have to do. We are in this together.

I look forward to the weekend, but before I even begin the drive home, I am aware of my energy and happiness. I am laughing and sharing time with my students, something that only a season or two earlier would never have happened. In this state of mind I am free, released from dread, to meander in fields of thought where I have not played in for years.

I remember when Dad worked two jobs for over a year, to save our house while Mom was sick for the first time. Bleary-eyed and ghostly, he never wavered, never faltered. I remember him going out the door into the black to work the night shift, despite wanting to be with his family. He was our hero. The work ethic he instilled in me still exists.

I am sure it is going to be a good weekend, but I do not realize how great. As is my custom it begins with a solo morning run, followed by a seriously large lunch, then a family excursion on mountain bikes. At nightfall we are home, tired and at peace, always a good place to be, both mentally and physically. I know that all too soon I will be waiting late into the night for my daughter to come home safely from a date, or my sons from a night of howling at the moon.

I pushed hard during my Saturday run, and since Sunday is born hot, I jog instead of my usual running pace. To balance this I add distance. It is remarkable what a different experience and perspective one receives by altering one's pace. Later, in the magic shower, I realize how true that is about life's pace as well.

After Sunday's lunch, the family leaves for the kid's soccer game and I have permission for some deserved Dad time. I am going to spend this sacred time watching a baseball game. I enter the kitchen in search of the beer that is beckoning from the fridge. Opening the fridge door, I spy the little guy who is willing to sacrifice himself, but on the way to the couch we somehow end up in the backyard.

The near end of the spring day just wills me to the hammock. I lie on my back gazing at the treetops, and put my untouched beer on the freshly mowed grass. Lab trots over and, with a grunt, lies under me in the shade. The smell of grass reminds me of all the shared family activities. Games of catch with kids and dogs, picnics, leaf raking, gardening, barbecues, and marriage-testing shed-building are all fond recollections of days past.

I watch ravens trying to drive an eagle to ground, nipping at the magnificent bird's feathers. The eagle soars and the ravens dive. I cover my eyes from the sun's glare. When they fly directly into the brightest section of the sky, I am forced to look away. I follow the action by watching the shadows circling and darting along the grass. The intensely black shadows appear to represent the eternal struggle between good and evil. Order and chaos plays out in the clear blue skies. One tries to soar high while the other attempts to drive it to ground. I refocus and look up just as the great eagle angles its wings allowing it to land at the top of a one-hundred-and-twenty-foot tree. The ravens persist in their swooping attacks, but the regal head of the bald eagle refuses to acknowledge their pitiful efforts.

Then it happens, my third epiphany. My eyes are slowly following the trunk of the tree that the eagle claims. The tree appears to tremble, and a single leaf floats down. I notice it because it is spring and few leaves fall this time of year. It drifts in slow motion. I wonder what became of the leaf that earlier in the year had raised its twin anchors, dread and fatigue, allowing it to blow on down the road. I conjecture that perhaps this is where the wind has blown it. It floats first left then right. It drops two feet in an instant, and then just hangs suspended until deciding to fall some more. Then it flitters wherever the warm breeze takes it. One leaf has blown on down the road and another is aimlessly meandering. Soon the falling leaf will join its brethren in the world of gone.

Then I realize it! My third epiphany touches me not emotionally or psychologically but in the part of my make-up where reality exists. While watching the leaf fall, I understand that sometimes leaves fall on days just like today. But not like today at all!

It will never be exactly this way, ever again. In fact, I have not had a day just like today ever before, and never will in the future. This day, this moment, has not and never will happen again. This is it! Life is moments, and each moment is perfect and divine, and will never repeat. In all the eons of human existence, none will see this particular moment. In all the stars and all the galaxies, this specific moment will never happen again.

Even if the theories of some scientist are accurate, in all the multiple universes and all the various dimensions, this moment will never be again. In all the ages past and the eons to come, that leaf will never fall that way again—not exactly, like this. These are my moments, my days, seen by no one the way that I perceive them. With no ego, I am allowed to see. The moments that make up my life are mine and mine alone.

With this realization, I watch the leaf touch upon the grass and at the same moment a shadow streaks across the ground. I look up to see the eagle soaring. Fittingly, there are no ravens in sight to impede the eagle's flight. Perfect timing. I understand how blessed my life has been, even when I did not know it. I also realize how spiritual every moment of every human's journey is. We all experience the unique moment in our own unique way.

Looking back at the tree, I am aware that I have never really seen it before. I have looked at it, but never seen it. Everything looks different—not better or worse, just different. It is all so perfect, so simple. In my wonder of a leaf, I find simplicity and perfection. I find the moment. This is it!

While waiting for my family to return, I make some calculations and soon have the makings of a dynamic lesson for first period Monday. The noise from the front of the house reveals that the victorious soccer players have returned. It is then that I acknowledge my third epiphany is without pain. This is possibly the first time that I have learned without the assistance of pain. In fact, it is a remarkably peaceful experience. Thinking back, I believe it is the first time in my life that learning has not involved dread. Maybe I truly am evolving. Where this specific evolutionary process is going, I am unsure. The one thing that I do know now is that every moment of this journey will be precious to me.

I drive to work Monday morning, confident I have a lesson that will defeat the powerful first period snores. When the students shuffle in, they are greeted with the number 36,500 on the blackboard. I ask the bleary-eyed students what that number represents. There are predictably no answers, but I am pleased that some students are at least thinking. The class clown earns a chuckle as he snickers, "The number of days before we get out of this jail?"

I explain. "That number represents the number of days an individual has on this planet if they live to be one hundred years old. That is all, 36,500 days! And remember, most people live only until eighty."

A few heads pop up and stare at the blackboard. I share with them that a friend's father died at age sixty-six, meaning he lived for roughly only 24,350 days—mind boggling. I then point out that most of the people sitting in this room have already lived about six thousand of their days. It is fulfilling to see calculators come out in disbelief. It becomes oddly quiet in the room until a student blurts, "Then why are we wasting time in school?"

The class and I laugh, then I explain, "But you need to be here to learn how many days you have in your life." I finish the lesson by adding, "Welcome to your journey—and just so you know, it's an honor to be a part of it." A few faces smile back.

Penny is listening but her fingers continue to manipulate her calculator. She takes my lesson to a deeper place. She announces, "The girl who died used only 6,666 of her days." Her voice drops to a whisper. "She still had 29,834 days left."

The train whistle blows "MOVE!" signifying the next station is at hand. Not one of the passengers in my section moves. We all sit, pensive.

I break the silence. "Use your days; be sincere, be genuine, take nothing for granted, treat others well, treat yourself well, be great." I have actually slowed the pace of the train and have to remind my students that the next station waits. The student's stream out and it is obvious that they are all thinking.

Penny walks slowly past and says, "That was a great lesson. Thanks." Waves of sheer elation sweep over me, yet I feel small and humble. I have made a commitment to give Penny hope, but in return, hope touches me. The moment is exquisite. My day number 14,708 is perfect. Somewhere, a single leaf is gliding to the earth, and I hope that someone notices.

Chapter 25

When people reach the highest perfection, it
is nothing special; it is their normal condition.
~Hindu Saying

The last few days of spring are special, and of course unique.
Penny keeps her word and attends every day. I spend time talking with students between classes, and continue meeting my
troll-student once a week under the stairs. When the weekend
begins, I am aware that summer waits on the other side. Soon
after its arrival will come the golden time of holidays.

Saturday promises that soon the summer's heat will
arrive. Thankfully, the smells remain pure spring. During the
year, I always look forward to this very day. The neighbors and
my family dread the day, and I am sure they think strangely
of me for being so excited. It is firewood delivery day, and this
means a full day behind the wheelbarrow. In the country, firewood orders are placed in the spring or summer and not, as we
learned in our first year, during winter. This was another lesson
that came hard, as that first winter was cold. A very sad sight
indeed is the cold empty hole of a fireplace unused in the middle
of a snowstorm.

My anticipation of the day is partially due to the security

that firewood represents; because of it, no storm-induced power failure will leave my family shivering. The family's perspective is less on security and more on a hard day's work.

The truck arrives, and everyone jumps to the chores like a well-oiled machine. Well, I jump; everyone else complains with comments like "Dad's weird," and "Not again this year." Despite my taking the high road and ignoring them, the shuffling feet are a less than silent mutiny. In time, my sons and I bulldoze wheelbarrow loads of wood up the trail to the back yard shed. Mother and daughter stack the cords high while between loads they dash inside and bake bread. Lab's duties are to bound about, annoying and tripping everyone in sight. He is the only family member who goes about his chores with the same relish as I do. Since everyone else will scoff at me, I share one thought with the only family member who understands. During a rest-break I ask Lab, "Does it get any better than this? A spectacular day, physical work, family together and bread baking in a log home." Lab's disposition indicates that he agrees, but when he waves a paw in the air, he reminds me that I have forgotten to add one thing to make the day perfect. When he is right, he's right. I whip inside and bring out a dog treat.

Break is over and I resume the grunts of effort, willing the loaded wheelbarrow up the trail. My mind drifts, helping to ignore the effort to keep the entire load from shoving me back down the hill. Summer is only two days away and school is almost over, the great train is nearly spent, as are so many of its passengers and employees. The changes I have experienced and at times endured have touched the very core of who I am. Three epiphanies have changed me from "Shadow" to an entity that can acknowledge its true self. This process takes place in the land of choice, where free will chooses how learning opportunities are used, or not. This gives me "Substance."

While sweating with effort, I reminisce about the first epiphany that seems so long ago, as if experienced by another person, some other fellow that lived in another time. It is not unlike how adults feel when they look back upon their childhood: familiar memories, but at the same time oddly foreign.

I have been unconscious, traveling through time and space with no meaning. I have innumerable learning opportunities, but am disappointed at how little actual learning occurs. My epiphany knocks down survival walls, making room for the wisdom needed to take baby steps toward consciousness. Survival is not what life is about. At this time, life for me is a paradox. To exist, life must be embraced. For me to embrace life, I need to exist.

The second epiphany, like the first, came from a place of pain. It brought forth a deeper understanding of reality. It is at this time that I abandon my "Shadow," separated from it by a force of nature, the will of reality. My ego became less, and I travel the gray area between unconsciousness and consciousness in the land called choice. With a smaller ego, I evolve from existing to caring, first about myself and then for others.

I am well into the third cord of wood when I think of my third epiphany. This is the only epiphany not involving pain, and potentially indicates that I am evolving. This epiphany reveals that life is simple and not complex. Every moment is sacred and unique. In all time and space, no two moments are exactly alike, yet simple moments make up life. First, there is existence, then caring and finally the moment. This is it!

My wise sons are taking a deserved nap under a willow, using Lab as a pillow. I cannot tell who snores louder. Their noise interrupts my thought and I become aware of my wheelbarrow and the strain. Mother and daughter are drinking juice on the balcony. It is time to rest. At the top of the trail, I lower the wheelbarrow and we both groan in agreement.

I smile with the realization it is time to leave the land of choice. Ironic that it is not a choice to leave but a realization, one where my three epiphanies have guided me. When I cried river rocks, I was making room within, so that I could exist. The ice storm forced me to deal with reality, and the only cognizant choice to make when faced with reality is to care. Existence leads to caring, which guides to the moment. Every moment is divine and perfect. Only in how we perceive it do we choose to label the lesson good or bad. As "Substance," I know who I am and what I believe in, and with that simple moment, consciousness becomes my normal condition.

When an individual truly exists, they must care. Wherever there is caring, there is hope. With hope walks consciousness. As "Substance," I am aware that there now will be less free will, less choice, because life will now be simple, but not simpler. As "Substance," consciousness rules and I simply no longer have access to denial.

With a groan, the wheelbarrow and I return to our task. My wife shouts from the deck chair, "You love this day, don't you?"

With sweat dripping off my nose, my answer is simple. "Yes."

While toiling, I conclude that consciousness does not lead to a world without problems. It does however, lead to a life of peace. A great life must entail peace. Greatness for me, combined with effort, manifests within my family and in my chosen field, education. For someone else, it may manifest another way or in any other area of life.

While I'm working, the staff meeting from the previous week keeps playing in my head. The train conductors claim our train has, again this year, attained greatness. I no longer accept this. The reality is that truth does not change to time; time changes to truth. If I live consciously, reality will manifest.

Time will manifest, just as the lotus blossom, in perfect bliss. There is no good or bad, only what must manifest for "Shadow" to become "Substance."

During the staff meeting, we discuss school goals and mission statements for next year. It is apparent that our effort is to be so vague that we cannot be held accountable. We spend hours collaborating on mission statements, chiseling each word until the sentence says nothing. Putting the humanity into teaching is difficult enough without this superficiality. I find this unbelievably painful to watch, and observe my mentor's anguish. He chooses then to whisper the question he asked me a lifetime ago: "Why so many secretaries and so few counselors?"

Deep down, I know the answer. Bureaucracy drives the train. Children's needs do not. I do not have to answer his question, as he knows that I know.

Then he adds something that makes all that I perceive irrelevant. With my ego dead, the unimportant becomes unimportant. "There is no place I would rather be than here, right now, in this moment, teaching. I will cherish my moments and value the passengers on this train."

I ask, "How is that possible, knowing what you know?"

His eyes dance. "My train rides on rails of hope, and it has but one destination… consciousness."

When I was lazy, I contributed to the unconsciousness of this train. Once, I too rode the rails of bureaucracy to the end of the year. But now, I understand that evolution also involves forgiving oneself. I am more than the sum of my worst actions. To move on, one must get past what they used to be and acknowledge who they want to be, so that in time they become exactly that. Consciousness is difficult to hold onto, and I must work hard to maintain my moment.

It takes an entire day to store the wood, but once it's

completed, I have a deep sense of accomplishment. My family is prepared for the coming of a far-off winter. Sunday sleep comes easily, and before drifting off I consider what an incredible spring I have experienced. The entire cycle that occurs during the season, from flowers to consciousness, is enlightening. I am ready for the golden time of summer. I am conscious and evolved. I am looking forward to the moments of everyday, to every day's moment! This is it! What beyond this can summer possibly bring?

Spirit: A vital force that characterizes a living being as being alive.

You must be the change you wish to see in the world.
~Mahatma Gandhi

Chapter 26

We begin from the recognition that all beings cherish happiness and do not want suffering. It then becomes both morally wrong and pragmatically unwise to pursue only one's happiness oblivious to the feelings and aspirations of all others who surround us as members of the same human family. The wiser course is to think of others when pursuing our own happiness.

~Tenzin Gyatso

It takes weeks for me to decompress from the train's pace. Once it roars to its final station, coughing and gasping for air, there is a tired sigh of steam and then quiet. Success is declared.

The year ends as it began. No fanfare, no gradual slowing of pace: just a jolt, and it's over. People pile from the train. Smiles do not make it into eyes.

After a few days, I am able to find the moment. It comes quietly and in broad daylight. While I eat the blackberries that grow in my backyard like free candy and taste like sunshine, Lab trots past. His purple smile indicates how adept he is at curling back his lips to expose his teeth. Where other dogs do

171

this to snarl and intimidate, he does it to pick blackberries right from the bush.

It is that moment when I realize I am enjoying one of the most relaxing days of my life. In reality, it is beyond relaxing; peace has found its way to my backyard. Like the end of the school year, it does not come with fanfare. I just look and there it is.

With the simple consciousness of an uncluttered mind the moment manifests. In this moment, I reflect on the first days of summer, the last two days of school and the decision that I am forced to make: a choice between what is best for someone else and my own hopes and happiness.

I had taken Penny aside and broke the news to her. She has failed. I wanted and hoped that she would pass, particularly considering how hard she has worked.

From the very beginning, we had a pact; she attends every day, and I stand beside her. I want her to pass so that she experiences the pride of accomplishment. Higher than my hopes, however, is the reality that her best efforts are just not enough to earn the promotion. There is not enough time left in the school year for her to accomplish the necessary assignments.

It is disheartening when administrators and counselors pressure me to pass her. They had warned that the time needed to accomplish our goal might not be there... but since she is close... they want to move her along. They praise our efforts and, with the best of intentions, offer to "Bend the rules." But I know that will deny reality. If I break our pact, then I will be disrespecting all that transpired between us. It would simply make everything we did a lie! Penny and I had decided to walk together in the world of reality, and I have confidence that she will understand. I make the decision.

On the last day of school, I sit with her and break the

news. She listens stoically, while I explain that I am proud of her and if she wants me as her teacher next year it will be my honor. I wait for a response. There is none. I forge on, concerned that all the work we have done is turning into bad feelings. I take a deep breath. "You worked hard, but there just wasn't enough time. If I pass you, it won't be legitimate. We agreed that it must be real. I want you to consider being in my class in September. Maybe, you can get credit for the work you did this year, and not have to repeat the entire year." Instead of altering reality, I offer hope.

Finally she reacts, as only Penny can. Just before leaving she mutters, "I told you that you were going to make me think. We'll see."

I drive home that night with two boulders on my shoulders. "We'll see!"

Well into summer, I am shopping at the grocery store and try to ignore the shadows of tourists. I often wonder how people on holidays keep "the city intensity" on their faces. Here they are, straight off their boats and planes or simply out from their tents, yet the "head down, grasping something tightly in their hands with a scowl on their face" strategy still controls them.

The poor grocery clerks who are more accustomed to leisurely conversations about my kids, or sneaking a chocolate bar into my bag while saying, "Here's a little something for your child" look harassed by the invasion of urban refugees.

Now is definitely the time to take my family to the hidden place, the lake that only locals know, the one I did not hear about until I had lived in this little harbor for ten years. It is the lake that we go to whenever the tourists become overwhelming. The fifth lake in our area is a twenty-minute drive down an apparently abandoned dirt road. After four-wheel driving along a dried riverbed and up a small hill, the trail ends in the middle of nowhere. Only a small boulder painted sky blue gives away its location. After finding the hidden trail, the tradition is for whoever uses it last to cover the entrance with branches and scrub. A ten-minute hike is next, following a deer trail until the forest gives up its secret. The first locals called this place Lake Beautiful.

At the trail's end, the first sound we hear is a shouted "Hi," from our neighbors. The kids are off swimming before I can say "Have fun." Lab sees familiar wagging tails, and off he gallops before I can command "Stay." Oh well, I still have my loyal wife.

Apparently I spoke too soon, as she and some friends are hastily setting up planks as benches so a local guitarist can serenade. Alone, I find a quiet, semi-shaded area and enjoy the music that soon wafts over the lake. I am lost in thought when a familiar voice surprises me: "Hello." I shade my eyes and squint into the sun. I can make out the dark outline of a person standing above me. "Penny! How wonderful to see you."

Just then, Lab comes running over and leaps up to give Penny a hug while licking her face. He is so friendly he almost knocks her down. I begin to apologize but she cuts me off while giggling, "What a good dog. Where's your Frisbee?" He has been swimming and completely drenches her, but she seems oblivious and rubs his wet smelly fur as if they are long lost pals. How does she know Lab, and why does she think he has a Frisbee? This is extremely rare behavior for my dog. Despite his antics with the family, he is generally standoffish when it comes to strangers. We always joke that one must earn Lab's respect before he will show any acknowledgement. Uncharacteristically, he now sits at Penny's feet as she absent-mindedly pats his head. I look at my wife and it is clear that she too finds Lab's friendly demeanor odd. He simply does not take to strangers this way.

"How do you know about this place?" I ask.

"Lake Beautiful? I've been coming here ever since I was a baby."

"How are you doing?"

"Good. I was devastated with failing." Then she grins. "But as long as I know I have your support next year, I'll be fine." She has made the right decision!

I flush with pride. "I'll be right beside you."

Oddly, she adds. "Yes. You will be." With that, she beams an incandescent smile that makes it into her eyes, waves goodbye and vanishes into the forest. Most peculiar however, is that I have to call Lab back or he would have followed her.

My wife, with her great insight, says, "So that's Penny. Wow, she's a great kid."

I smile knowing that both Penny and her potential will be waiting patiently at their desk next September. A student can fail as long as we have earned their trust. It is all about caring. I believe that I will not see Penny again until summer is over and school begins.

I am so very wrong.

Chapter 27

When we quit thinking primarily about ourselves and our own self-preservation, we undergo a truly heroic transformation of consciousness.
~Joseph Campbell

Today, I take Lab on a flat jog around the lakes. The smell of lavender from butterfly bushes dominates the trail. The exquisite odor predictably attracts butterflies, which in turn brings out the even more predictable butterfly-chasing instincts of Lab. While pondering why he was so friendly with Penny, I find my stride is defined by how successful he is at tripping me.

Slowing my pace, I contemplate another incident with an animal. A few days earlier, I watched a caterpillar crawl across our deck and eventually onto my running shoe. Patiently carrying it out into the yard, I place it on the ground, then watch as it sits perfectly still. In time, it decides to move and I wonder what process a caterpillar goes through to choose that now is the time. Is there a genetically programmed time limit before the all-clear signal activates?

When it decides to move, of the three hundred and sixty degrees of choice, why does it choose to take the one exact degree of direction leading back to my foot? It never detours. None of the stones and weeds—that to the caterpillar are mountains and jungles—causes it to deviate. In wonderment I watch, as it reappears on the deck. Like an obsessed furry worm, its line never changes. I do what I felt is the only respectful thing; I place my feet back where they originally were.

The caterpillar has traveled about twenty feet and is now climbing back onto my running shoe exactly where it had been twenty minutes earlier. In this piece of fluff, how much consciousness is there? Climbing over my shoe, it continues fulfilling its destiny. Like the lotus blossom, with a small ego, knowing perfectly its bliss.

As Lab and I continue jogging, it is wonderfully relaxing. In these moments my mind clears. The little caterpillar takes on meaning that encourages me to continue my journey.

Later that evening, I share with my family the caterpillar story. My kids listen intently, and although the story ends with more questions than answers, I am proud of myself for having watched this small occurrence with awe. My wife listens, but seems more interested in watching the floatplanes taking off and landing in our harbor. I ask, "What are you thinking?"

"Sorry. I am listening, but I just wonder where everybody is going." She insightfully adds, "So many stories, so many adventures. Did I tell you that today I saw a four-foot tall sunflower on its side? Is there a sadder sight than the face of a sunflower lying on the ground?"

This made me appreciate the wonder of awe, and that again led to how does Penny know Lab? I accept that there is much more going on here than just my own consciousness. Just as the sun will eventually encourage the sunflower to stand, does the hope I offer also give Penny the confidence to try again? It seems however, that the more I offer hope, the more she somehow guides me.

I thought about a conversation I had in the last days of school. A new teacher searched me out for advice, and I shared my limited experience. She paid me a compliment by saying, "I can't believe anybody would have that quality of insight. Maybe someday I'll get there, but it seems a long way off." The bureaucracy has already worked its magic, forcing her to see only her mediocrity. She is, in fact, a great teacher trying to be good, but just not aware of it. The speed of the train, the constant declarations of greatness, it has the effect of making those involved strive for something that isn't real.

I wonder if next year I will earn the right to be a mentor. If this manifests, I will have to share memories of my mentor, drawing a line from then to now and providing direction to there.

With that beautiful thought, I hear a voice from somewhere deep inside whispering. "Penny really is a great kid." My mentor and my wife, the two people I respect the most in life, have said it—and now I know and accept it. Penny really is a great kid! Great without my help. Great without ever knowing me. It is only the needs of the train that says she is not great!

Then I finally understand. When I offered her hope, she had allowed me to. By my caring for her, she guided me to consciousness. All this time, Penny has been enlightening me. All this time I have been trying to figure out how to help her, while she already knew how to help me. Then it hit me!

When she and my mentor had talked about words being rocks, he had thanked her. She is his Spirit Guide!

Simplification: To make something less complicated or easier to understand.

Everything should be made as simple as possible, but not simpler.
~Albert Einstein

Chapter 28

Personally I am always ready to learn, although
I do not always like being taught.
~Winston Churchill

Life is an amazing journey. This is particularly true when one's mind is at peace. An uncluttered mind free of angst, dread and fatigue, holding just the right number of stones, can travel to amazing places. Harmony brings unlimited potential. By taking control of the pace of our journey, we acknowledge the potential for spectacular moments. When I existed as "Shadow" it was a day-to-day battle to survive. As "Substance" all moments will be cherished, but none more than the now.

Despite this growth, I am unaware that my amazing journey is about to become spectacular.

Naturally, it begins simply. I return from my morning run and, due to the heat, collapse into the backyard hammock, sweat streaming from my body. It is blissful, and I am one with the world. Well, at least one with my backyard. I have run well within my limits, yet my time has been exceptionally fast. I feel peace of mind.

While gently swaying in the hammock, I glance at the tree where my third epiphany occurred, and smile. Contemplating the harmony of my life, the summer breeze takes me to a beautiful place. I begin to doze.

Just as I fall asleep, out of the corner of my eye I see Lab bounding toward me. A train drops me off at its last station, just outside a large stadium. A sign at the top of the stadium reads, "Seek nay", and I know that this is no ordinary stadium. My destination rushes towards me and the sign suddenly says "Seek no more."

Can intentions manifest into reality? Somehow I know that an answer, and much more, is waiting inside the stadium. I can enter if I have earned and deserve the privilege of participation. Nevertheless, it is difficult to take the first step.

Suddenly, my hand is gently grasped. I turn and am shocked to see Penny. She speaks candidly. "I am your Spirit Guide. You have been trying to get here for so long. This year you struggled mightily. I am very proud of you."

These last stones are the most beautiful I have ever accepted.

Her hand coaxes me forward. "Give your ticket to The Gatekeeper. It's wondrous inside." Curiously, a ticket is in my other hand. It has one word stamped upon it. "CHOICE."

There are many other people around me, all moving slowly but with purpose. There is no rush. Their pace is in harmony with what they value. I stand before a huge Gatekeeper. No words are spoken, as he gazes deep into my soul. I ponder; if it is choice that manifests the ticket, what cashes it in? The Gatekeeper, in his finest James Earl Jones voice, gently booms, "Welcome."

Perception reveals that intention is what cashes the ticket. I am inspired to answer. "I want to be great."

The Gatekeeper accepts my ticket and calls to the heavens. "Your eyes are wide! Go and use them."

My Spirit Guide subtly allows me to enter first. I look over my shoulder and see her proud smile. She gestures for me to continue forward. My senses heighten; everyone appears at peace. Each individual, just like the lotus blossom, has a destination determined by self-actualization.

Suddenly, out of nowhere, dread overwhelms me! I do not belong here, and I definitely do not deserve this. Far in the distance I hear my Spirit Guide calling, "Everything is okay." Her rocks weigh me down and momentarily hold me in place. Eventually however, I discard them and flee. All the people around me are somehow more deserving, more spiritual. They have earned this and I have not.

I stare at my feet and feel the dreaded angst-dance begin, in first my left foot and then my right. I am returning to "Shadow." I flee for the exit. The intimidating sight of The Gatekeeper blocking my way focuses my angst. His friendly smile is gone. I must get out of this stadium! His mass is too great for me to shove aside, so I have no option but to stand before him waiting to see what happens next.

My Spirit Guide breathlessly catches up just as The Gatekeeper says, "Come back anytime; we're always here for you. If you want back in, just give me your ticket." He steps aside like a giant gate. While passing I gasp. "I'm very sorry." He guffaws. "For what? Being you?"

Outside I bend over, my hands on my knees, trying to breathe. When my eyes focus, I am baffled. In my hand is another ticket. It is oddly comforting to know that my Spirit Guide stands beside me. She has entered and left the stadium as easily as I come and go from my home.

She speaks first. "I apologize. That was my fault." I appreciate her kindness but know that the fault is mine. At this moment, she is the living embodiment of compassion.

"Thank you," I stammer sheepishly, "I am not deserving."

She smiles benevolently. "You need the assistance of The Ferryman."

"What?" When I look up I stare at my mentor.

She continues despite my slack-jawed expression. "Your mentor is here to help ferry you across. It is what he does."

"Across where?" I feebly ask.

She continues, smiling. "From here to there," nodding toward the stadium.

I want to groan. This is not good. "I can't go there. I am not worthy."

The Ferryman—my mentor—responds, his Scottish brogue familiar, "I am to help you from unconsciousness to consciousness. You have evolved from "Shadow" to "Substance." These are heavy rocks, or so I think. "And now you need to evolve from "Substance" to "Spirit." Heavy rocks become heavier.

I ask hesitantly. "How do you intend to help me do that?"

His answer brings me no relief. "By helping you with the two questions that one must answer for their intention to bloom." I inhale, waiting. "The questions are simple. What do you have to forgive yourself for, and to whom do you have to show compassion?" Heavy rocks become heavier boulders.

I think out loud, "What do I have to forgive myself for?" Then collapse from the weight of these boulders and begin mentally listing transgressions and unintentional slights. The list grows as I internally recite errors and misgivings from my past.

Thankfully, The Ferryman interrupts. "Think! Are these things really relevant?"

I think deeper, and my mind returns to my first epiphany—where I took baby steps and my ego became smaller, so that I could know what is truly important. The Ferryman appears to understand what I am thinking and smiles.

"That's it," I sigh. "I have to forgive myself for who I was! I have to forgive myself for being less than what I know I can be. That's what this year has all been about! I knew intuitively all along that I should be more. I just wasn't ready."

All the fatigue and angst and dread are all because a primal force called evolution knows that I was not reaching my potential. How could I like myself until I realized that I was just doing the best I could at that time? I am more than the sum of my worst actions! I intellectually knew this but had not fully accepted it, not until my heart understood. As I realize this, forgiveness washes through me.

"Simple," The Ferryman says. "Now answer, to whom do you need to show compassion?" I begin recalling people who may or may not have wronged me.

With a sigh my Spirit Guide interrupts. "If you want inside that stadium, you will have to be more than that."

My answer manifests. "I should be compassionate to everyone, at all times."

I glance at my Spirit Guide and wonder if she respects my answer, an answer that she embodies. She returns a benevolent smile and her eyes reveal that my response is good, but unfortunately what she says is, "The Ferryman will need more." She sighs, while patiently looking at the stadium.

Her obvious desire to be inside and participating focuses my consciousness. I look at The Ferryman and speak with confidence. "Thank you for your patience. I get it. I must have compassion for all living things, but most difficult is having compassion for myself." My heart finally understands. The Gods are not far away but, like potential, they sit eternally waiting.

The Ferryman grins. "See? Not complex."

Both my Spirit Guide and the Ferryman speak in unison.

"We are proud of you." Time again slows and consciousness places me before The Gatekeeper.

He greets me with his familiar voice and a friendly "Hello, it is good to see you again." Oddly, he is not quite as tall as I remember.

I shake his massive hand and say, "It is an honor to meet you," while feeling as if I am part of something, something bigger than myself.

As I hand him the ticket with "CHOICE" stamped upon it, the Gatekeeper shouts again to the heavens. "His eyes are wide! It is but a choice!" He leans over and quietly whispers, "Everybody gets a new ticket each day... just in case you choose to leave again." I appreciate his kind advice.

I turn to The Ferryman who has helped me cross from bystander to participant, and to my Spirit Guide who embodies compassion. "Thank you for everything." When I approach the stadium, it is Penny and my mentor who are standing beside me. The three of us enter together.

Chapter 29

Our demons are our limitations, which shut us off from the realization of the ubiquity of the spirit ... each of these demons is conquered in a vision quest.
~Joseph Campbell

To ease my transition they entered as my student and my friend; but once inside they transform back to my Spirit Guide and Ferryman. Others immediately recognize them, and come over with warm greetings. It is irrefutable that I am joining august company. Ascending stairs, I have a sense of the long forgotten anticipation of youth. I thought I remembered what it was like to be young, but I do not, not really. The demons that time gives to all adults trick us into thinking we remember what youth is like. However, this vision quest holds the potential to conquer demons, allowing me to feel once again like a child.

Just steps from the top, I hear the murmur and feel the energy of a huge crowd. It is electric. I see every type of person, from babies and octogenarians to families and couples. Even those who are alone do not seem lonely. It is clear from those attending that all ages, cultures, races and religions are welcome.

My foot lands on the last step, and I smell freshly cut grass. It is so bright that I shade my eyes and look away. Then The Gatekeeper's voice booms through my consciousness. "You have eyes; use them." I concentrate on my vision quest and behold a lush, green field, brightly lit by sunshine and blue sky. I turn to see if my Spirit Guide and Ferryman are near. What I see I cannot believe. Lab pushes his way between them and sits like a puppy. My Spirit Guide is casually petting his head. My first thought is, "Of course! How else could Penny and Lab have known each other?" Lab is so happy that his tail is wagging him. He takes my hand in his mouth and gently guides me to our seats. Is this what he has been doing, all those evenings when I return home and he takes me on a tour of our yard?

Suddenly, as the crowd's movement sweeps us along, I lose contact with Lab. Normally I would worry, but instead know intuitively that he is safe—just like when I let go of my children's hands at the Christmas craft fair.

The crowd settles as people take their seats in anticipation. Over the loudspeaker I hear John Lennon singing: *"Imagine all the people, living for today..."* It is peculiar that I have not noticed the music earlier. My vision quest is so powerful that I am paralyzed. I stare at the beauty of the field and the surrounding seats. It appears that a baseball game is about to begin.

My Spirit Guide whispers, "This is just how it manifests to you, so that your psyche can understand." She adds, "Others create images they recognize. See that old couple over there? They are at their son's wedding. The children high in the stands, they think that you are on their playground at the top of their slide." Movement slowly returns to my legs. The loudspeaker's song continues: *"You can see it if you try."*

The more I accept this, the younger I feel. With each

thought and feeling I have of childhood, a demon is conquered.

We find our seats, and the massive scoreboard spells out "Equidem exisistere." I ask The Ferryman, "What does that mean?"

"I don't speak Latin. You'll have to ask your Spirit Guide." I cannot tell if he is serious or joking but behind his smile I see a glimpse of my mentor. It brings a warm memory of how he would never take anything too seriously.

I ask my Spirit Guide, "Do you see the message on the scoreboard?"

"Of course. If you see it, I see it. It means, 'I exist.'"

I query The Ferryman, "Is it appropriate to ask, where is this place?"

"Does it have anything to do with Latin?"

"I don't think so."

"Then I can answer." He laughs and proceeds not to.

"Well?" I ask. There is still no response. I clear my throat and ask a little louder, "This place, where is it?"

"Sorry," he mutters, "I just love watching your dog."

I turn as Lab leaps like a young pup high into the air. He is in the center of the field catching Frisbees tossed by the crowd. I mumble to no one, "I didn't know he could do that." His play is the focal point of the crowd's attention.

My Spirit Guide interjects. "What you're watching is how the stadium manifests for Lab. He's catching Frisbees tossed by children on a playground, by adults at a wedding, at a ballpark, and wherever else people think they are. I can see your manifestation because I'm your friend. Lab can see all of our manifestations because we are all his friends. He is a pack animal. In his pack he's the joker, the one that gets everybody else playing and having fun." I laugh realizing that is exactly what he does with our family. "It's somewhat unusual, but his consciousness allows him to see much more of what is happening at this moment than most of the people here. I think it is because he has fewer demons, so he is closer to the oneness of his spirit. In his consciousness he is chasing Frisbees, and in their consciousness they are being entertained —just as you are now." An ovation erupts after a particularly difficult catch. I laugh and applaud like a child.

I turn to The Ferryman, who is gently humming along with John Lennon, *"Imagine no possessions."* But he stops when I ask, "Will you answer my question now?"

"Only if you remember what it is."

"Where is this place?" I ask.

"This place is inside you. It's where your consciousness exists."

"Where in me is that?"

His answer surprises me. "Point at yourself." I point. "Everybody always points at the identical place. When you point at yourself you are saying, this is me, this is where I exist. You didn't point at your brain or your stomach. You pointed at the same place the man from China points to, or the woman from Africa. You point to your existence, where your consciousness is." My finger is pointing directly at my heart.

Without warning, my vision quest transforms into the round table where my mentor and I used to meet once a month. With that, the stadium speaker's song changes as well. Louis Armstrong's voice is now croaking melodically. *"I see trees of green, red roses too, I see them bloom, for me and you."* From our table we still have a breathtaking view of the field. The Ferryman pats me on the back and muses, "That's better, more intimate. Now I can tell that you are relaxing."

I watch animated conversations and small pockets of regulars who swap stories of grandeur. The song continues. *"I see friends shaking hands, saying how do you do, they're really* saying, I... love... you." Some people sit in plush armchairs, looking as if they have been coming to this event for generations. Others have expressions of peace that make me conclude they have visited here for eons. They mouth the words to Mr. Armstrong's song. *"I see skies of blue, and clouds of white, the bright blessed day, the dark sacred night."* Others sit like me, with eyes wide.

I turn to The Ferryman, take a deep breath and ask, "You say this is where I exist, where I am conscious, but what exactly is that?"

"It is the place of the bigger horizon."

My Spirit Guide interjects. "First you make your ego smaller, then you exist, then the moment manifests."

The Ferryman continues, "Yes, exactly, the moment. That's what this place is, it's the moment."

My conscious and unconscious do a collective "Huh?"

The Ferryman laughs. "I'll try again. You evolve making your ego small. You have accomplished that. Every conscious person earns a ticket every day through opportunities and choices. It can be lost, ignored, ripped up, or thrown away, but it immediately reincarnates. Once earned, intention cashes the ticket. This allows you inside your moment. Some, like you, struggle with this lesson. But fortunately the lesson is always there, waiting." I thought of the potential that sits waiting for each child. "My job is to ferry you from unconsciousness to consciousness. I assist individuals from outside to inside—inside their moment. Do you understand?" My blank expression reveals my answer. The Ferryman patiently adds, "What is this place? It is the place inside you where consciousness exists." He spreads his arms wide and concludes. "This is the home of consciousness. It... your perception of the moment, it manifests here. This is where evolution happens." He points at my

191

heart and says, "Inside, here, is where substance prevails over shadow."

I am oddly serene. "I get it. First, I am an observer of the moment, then, if earned through my intentions, I can actually interact with the moment, and that is when the opportunity to evolve is present." The Ferryman and my Spirit Guide smile, so I ask. "Then what?"

My Spirit Guide's answer is typically simple. "We'll see."

I hesitate then ask. "Ferryman, earlier you explained that the lotus blossom attains bliss because it knows that it is a lotus blossom. Remember I joked that it did not act like a cat?"

He nods, so I continue, "How do you know that the lotus blossom actualizes its bliss with every morning incarnation?"

He glances cautiously at my Spirit Guide and hesitates before answering. "If, for you, there is something beyond "Substance" then all will be made clear. But that my friend, is for you to discover." The song on the speakers ends. *"And I think to myself... what a wonderful world."*

My Spirit Guide interrupts. "It's about to begin!" I turn excitedly toward the field, and the brightness dims. The crowd hushes, and silence envelopes the stadium. We wait. Nothing happens. We wait longer and still, nothing. I look at my Spirit Guide and The Ferryman who are intently watching the field.

I wait even longer, and for even longer, nothing happens. I lean over and whisper to my Spirit Guide. "What happens next?"

"Next," she said, "I don't understand."

Slightly frustrated I explain, "Well nothing is happening."

While gazing past me she says rather confused. "Are you sure?"

The Ferryman interjects. "If this is your consciousness manifesting itself, have you asked, why are these other people here? What is their purpose in your manifestation, and what is yours in theirs?"

I recognize the odd face. There is the janitor who salts the parking lot each morning. A few rows over, my neighbor sits. Farther away I recognize the mechanic from the local garage. Mainly, however, there are strangers in the tens of thousands.

While thinking how odd this is, our round table manifests in the center of the grass field. Despite feeling uncomfortable with everyone looking down at us, something deep in my heart reveals that I might be getting it. Yet, doubt overwhelms me.

I turn to my Spirit Guide and ask. "Penny... please... help me. What is happening here? I am losing touch with reality! Why are we sitting in the middle of the field?"

She calmly answers. "Losing touch with reality? No... I don't think so. You are actually touching reality. Your perspective is changing. Relax... this is just your first vision quest. Every religion and culture has some form of this. It is amazingly common. Everyone experiences this, although few realize it." Within my heart, the sense that I understand grows.

From somewhere above the stadium The Gatekeeper's voice booms. "Your eyes are open; use them."

The Ferryman chimes in, "Concentrate! Use your consciousness. As your father asked of you, think—all the time." Just then, I think I see Dad walking with someone. Their backs are to me as they stroll out of sight. Was that actually Mom, and were they holding hands? How is that possible? My heart, the center of my consciousness, bursts. "I get it!"

Seeing my Mom makes me feel even younger, and more conquered demons fall thrashing to the ground. They fall like the rocks of my first epiphany, the ice pearls of my second epiphany and the leaf of my third epiphany.

Inspired, my spirit soars. For the first time I listen to my heart. It is not just about my moment. It is about the moments of all the others! That is why all these strangers are here. They offer me an opportunity to be compassionate. I look around and truly belong. Our hearts, our consciousness, is joined together by the moment.

Substance understands; everything affects everything. The butterfly beating its wings on the other side of the planet really does affect me. In that moment, every person in attendance sees my consciousness manifest. I become spirit. They applaud just as I see their awareness and stand to acknowledge them. I am one with the everyday heroes who make life worth living. The Gods are near.

Then my Spirit Guide explains as only she can. "Now you know why compassion is so important. Once you are conscious and realize we are all one, how can you act any other way than compassionately."

The Ferryman continues. "If every moment is an opportunity for consciousness, and everything affects everything, then being compassionate in all moments is consciousness."

My Spirit Guide simplifies. "Consciousness has a power because it can manifest into reality. When you are compassionate to one you are compassionate to all, including yourself. Likewise, when you are kind to yourself, all will share the benefit. That is why it is so important to forgive oneself, so that all may benefit. Forgiving yourself is not done for you; it is done for them. This is what makes our intentions so important, and why we must understand our own hearts. Why we must become spirit." These words are the size of mountains.

My Spirit Guide continues. "For us to evolve, we must be conscious of why we do things. If our hearts manifest reality and we don't understand why we do something, if we just do things because we can, the results most likely will be disastrous." I knew that the next words would be continent size.

"For the human race to blossom, we must understand where all the hatred and revenge comes from, and not just react to it. We must understand the intentions of our heart. The change must come from inside us, in our hearts. Inside our moments, revenge propagates revenge; from compassion blooms compassion. It is but a choice."

The Ferryman adds. "See simple, not complex. The Gods are closer than we realize. They reside in every compassionate act. For you, it was the thought of losing Penny that stimulated your evolution. You care, and that defines who you are. Imagine you have the most important meeting you will ever attend. Your life, your happiness, everything depends on making this meeting. Nothing will stop you from making that meeting. Then imagine your pocket is full of pennies and you have a hole so that one penny falls out, you will never stop to fix the hole or pick up the penny. Your meeting is far too important. But somewhere on your journey to your meeting, a meeting upon which your own happiness depends, there is a number—a number of pennies that, if you lose enough, you will stop to fix the hole—no matter how important the meeting. For you, this Penny stopped you. You made her more important than your own destination. You stopped to help her, and because of that, found peace and discovered harmony. You experienced compassion. You lived in the moment.

"From when a leaf falls, or an epiphany happens, to noticing a hummingbird, this is where it occurs; here is where it exists, where we are conscious—in our hearts. The manifestation of my intentions is directly a reflection of my heart. The opportunity for compassion exists." The Ferryman concludes. "Simple."

I mutter, "It begins and ends inside me. I learn what the child already knows, and we as adults have lost. As a teacher, if I want to help others learn, it is not about my moment; it is about their moment. If I want to influence, I must build a relationship from my moment to their moment. Then I will have influence. Every time that I deal with just their behavior I lessen our relationship, but to influence behavior I must have a relationship. There must be a 'we', not just a 'you.' This applies to all relationships from the baby to its mother, from the teacher to the student, from the principal to the staff, from one country to another, from me to God."

The Ferryman adds, "From the mentor to the apprentice."

I nod.

"Then," my Spirit Guide whispers, "this vision quest is over."

There is no fanfare: just perfect reality. We stand to leave, and thousands of people appear content. I look back at the field and realize that I have been in the moment. I have gazed upon my heart where consciousness exists. My heart is nothing but a reflecting pool of my intentions. At first it is terrifying, then less so, and finally beautiful. Much like life itself.

The stadium speakers come to life, but I cannot place who is singing. *"It's a beautiful morning, I think I'll go outside for awhile, and just smile."*

Next I find myself standing in front of The Gatekeeper, who grins and looks deep into my heart. He says, "I see that your quest is successful. I am happy." His massive body moves and as I pass he whispers, "Remember, every day you have a choice." He adds something that I do not hear.

"What did you say?" I ask.

He smiles, and with a twinkle of knowledge in his eyes, answers. "I said, till we meet again my friend. Take what your journey offers, be thankful, and don't lose what you have."

Again I hear his laughter as I thank him, and in anticipation of my next vision quest I add, "I am grateful for your patience." Then I speak a word that I have never used before; I wave and say, "Godspeed."

Once outside the stadium, I continue to hear the song. *"It's your chance to wake up and plan another brand new day, either way, it's a beautiful morning."* A ticket marked CHOICE has reincarnated in my hand.

Penny grins. "If I don't see you before, I'll be in your class next week." Her smile tells me that if I need my Spirit Guide, she will be there. She touches my hand, and I feel a piece of paper slip into it. I assume this is how I have been getting the tickets. "Curious," I thought, "I already have one." With that she turns and just walks away.

As the crowd disperses I can still hear the stadium speakers. *"It just ain't no good if it's sunshine and you're still inside, shouldn't hide, seems to me that people keep seeing more and more each day. Lead the way, it's okay."*

My mentor jokes, "You were a most difficult apprentice." I smile, knowing that consciousness is hard to hold on to, but if I falter, The Ferryman will be there to help. He shakes my hand. "I'll see you soon." For all of us, these understated goodbyes will make it easier the next time we meet. With this simple ending, my first vision quest is complete. My remarkable year is nearly over.

The seasons have come and gone. The circle is nearly closed, and what remains are the lessons learned. Memories merge into hopes as I have grown from "Shadow" to "Substance" to "Spirit." Within the seasons of the year, I have had the privilege of enduring opportunities. I have walked in the realm of choice, and been forced to grow.

Out of my journey comes one simple reality: we are our intentions. What we intend to happen, be it good or bad, blossoms every day—and we live with the consequences of that. For some, it may well be easier to remain asleep and unconscious, but they will certainly miss the vitality and essence of life. The unconscious will never be capable of declaring their intentions, and therefore the change that they hope and dream will not be brought forth. Then frustration and fatigue soon begin the cycle that causes dread to dominate. Even in this state, potential waits patiently. The lesson stands available. Despite unconsciousness, dread can still motivate us to participate.

Just before I return to my home and hammock, a memorable voice booms from the serenity of my heart. "It is but a choice!"

How blessed I am to have a Ferryman like my mentor, to ease the journey from here to there, and Penny, my Spirit Guide, who helped me find substance. Like the lotus blossom in the early morning, their intentions flowered.

Thinking of Penny reminds me of the piece of paper she slipped into my hand. I reach into my pocket and pull it out. I read it and smile. Folding it, I place it back in the pocket nearest my heart. I will cherish this nugget of gold for my next evolutionary step. It is at the center of balance, the change I want in this world: "Simplify!"

Epilogue

Before enlightenment
chopping wood
carrying water.

After enlightenment
chopping wood
carrying water.

~Zen Proverb

My vision quest manifested while I dozed in the hammock. While still waking, I receive a clear understanding of what the word "Godspeed" means: an entire life lived in a conscious moment. In a flash, I have evolved. I remember it all, the epiphanies, the seasons and the stadium. "Shadow" is unaware of the moment, "Substance" can participate in the moment, and "Spirit" *is* the moment!

I even vaguely remember seeing Lab out of the corner of my eye. Suddenly, I am fully awake and he races to a stop, drops his Frisbee and startles me by licking my face. The world spins upside down, as sky becomes ground and ground, sky.

Spun from the hammock, I lay with my head on the ground, feet tangled in the hammock, and my first thought is, "Where did he get the Frisbee?"

Just then, my wife enters the back yard. She is returning to give me a forgotten good-bye kiss. With my feet still twisted in the hammock and Lab bounding about, she laughs, "That's not very dignified."

I make unseemly grunting sounds while struggling to unravel myself. I try and fail to save my dignity. Finally I untangle and, with an awkward thump, find gravity and the world rights itself.

With a dumbfounded expression she asks, "What in the world have you and Lab been doing? Playing frisbee?"

I answer. "Well, actually, yes."

"I wanted to kiss you good-bye before I left. It appears you two are having an interesting time."

"Interesting... well, yes. It's amazing what quiet contemplation can do."

She corrects, "Or even play," then kisses me and, with a wink and a wave, leaves.

Lab and I continue our aborted game of catch, and I think to myself of how one simple conscious moment can be life-changing.

Tomorrow I will go into school early, as I do every year. I want to be well prepared for the start of the coming year, as I am every year. This year, however, I not only know that potential waits in each and every desk, but that my own potential also waits patiently.

There is only one thing left for me to do before this moment is done; Lab and I go for a walk. At the lake's shoreline I feel light. As sun sets, I skip rocks on the surface, imagining giving back the last of the words I carry with me. When I board the train tomorrow, I want my heart to be light so that I can fly to my dreams. I stop when I remember Penny's warning. "Some words are necessary for balance." What had my mentor repeated in the stadium? Yes, those would be rocks I keep. *"Simple, not complex."* I place three small, smooth stones in my pocket and stroll home.

~Namaste

Acknowledgments

The genesis of all books is a fascinating process. Seldom does that inspiration come from one mind, one source. While hiking the aptly named Golden Ears Mountain and resting on a small log in the middle of a massive rain forest, we came up with the idea for this novel. But from idea to creation there are many who deserve recognition.

First, appreciation goes to our families, to whom we dedicated this project; then our publisher Grey Gate Media, publicist Madi Predda, and especially the Cover Artist, Creative Director and Acquisitions Editor Pam Marin-Kingsley. Thank you Pam for your time, talent, and patience.

And most of all, we would like to thank the thousands and thousands of students, parents, counselors, caretakers, youth workers, support staff, administrators, and especially the dedicated teachers whom we have had the privilege of knowing. Their energy and passion have inspired this book. To all of you—many thanks.

A special acknowledgment goes to Mickey the Lab, who is no longer with us. Jeff ... he was always sorry about the day he bit your favorite hiking shirt.

Last and by no means least, one other person must be acknowledged—Penny. Her name is changed but her inspiration is true. To know the whole story, we must share the horrific, if for no other reason than to inspire.

Penny was a lovely little girl in elementary school, bubbly, giggling, curious and kind. She returned home for lunch one day just as her father committed suicide. He bled to death as Penny sat holding his hand.

She stopped talking after that and all enthusiasm for life was gone. The school rallied to her—she deserved nothing less. The principal dedicated every lunch hour to reading stories to her. Staff adjusted classes, lessons, their after school time, everyone, including students and support staff, stepped up.

Not a word was uttered by Penny for ten months.

One day, the students and parents were putting on a tea for the staff, Penny was there, silently bringing tea to any who asked. Out of nowhere and completely unexpectedly, her little voice was heard. She was standing next to me and said, "Would you like some tea?" For a moment she startled everyone, not because she spoke, it had come naturally when she was ready, but because her mother dropped her tea cup and rushed to hug her. Not a staff member had a dry eye.

When Penny finally completed her schooling and graduated with her grade twelve, I, along with principal, and staff, stood at the back of the auditorium as she bounced across the stage to receive her diploma. Her giggles and smile touched our hearts and inspired this story.

About the Authors

Jeff Leitch

Jeff Leitch lives with his family in Maple Ridge, a proud community at the base of the majestic Golden Ears Mountain in British Columbia, Canada.

Honored to be a teacher in his native Coquitlam, British Columbia, Jeff's passions include his wife Linda, their three kids, Amanda, Matthew and Adam, his Dad and Mom (always), brothers Greg and James, in-laws Pauline and Joe, his teammates, colleagues, friends, and the countless stories they all share. You can find him at any sporting venue or live theatre, with coffee in hand, cheering and coaching those who display courage and dare to chase greatness.

Along with writing occasional articles for local papers, Jeff's current restlessness has him dreaming of many more novels, while writing at least one musical hit as he goes beyond the three chords he knows on his acoustic guitar.

Roy Dimond

Roy Dimond, author of **The Singing Bowl** and **The Rubicon Effect** has collaborated with his long time friend, Jeff Leitch to create his first work of non-fiction, **Saving Our Pennys**.

Roy has worked for over thirty years as a Youth Worker within numerous school districts and over twenty schools. He has also spoken at universities about school culture, family violence, depression, and bullying.

Roy lives with his wife of many years in a small harbor called Garden Bay on the West Coast of British Columbia and is working on his next manuscript.

CPSIA information can be obtained at www.ICGtesting.com
Printed in the USA
LVOW13s1434130414

381505LV00003B/522/P